Migrants, Asylum Seekers, and Refugees:

A Euro-African

Problem in the 21st Century

The Relevance of 'Sollicitudo Rei Socialis'

Migrants, Asylum Seekers, and Refugees: A Euro-African Problem in the 21st Century

The Relevance of 'Sollicitudo Rei Socialis'

Chigozie Nnebedum

Globethics.net Focus No. 58

Globethics.net Focus Series

Publications Director: Prof. Dr Obiora Ike, Executive Director of Globethics.net in Geneva and Professor of Ethics at the Godfrey Okoye University Enugu/Nigeria.
Series Editor: Dr Ignace Haaz, Managing Editor

Globethics.net Focus Series
Chigozie Nnebedum, *Migrants, Asylum Seekers and Refugees: A Euro-African Problem in the 21st Century*
Geneva: Globethics.net, 2021
ISBN 978-2-88931-387-7 (online version)
ISBN 978-2-88931-388-4 (print version)

Managing Editor: Dr Ignace Haaz
Assistant Editor: Nefti Bempong-Ahun

Globethics.net International Secretariat
150 route de Ferney
1211 Geneva 2, Switzerland
Website: *www.globethics.net/publications*
Email: *publications@globethics.net*

All web links in this text have been verified as of February 2021.

TABLE OF CONTENTS

INTRODUCTION

The ability to move is one of the qualities of living organisms. Movement is occasioned by many factors ranging from the most sublime to the most nebulous. Human beings have utilized this quality to its fullest more than any other living creature on earth, either as a way of adapting to the changing situations in which they constantly find themselves or as an action resorted to in combating the threats to their existence. Such threats are usually not unconnected to their lives either directly or indirectly. This is the activity technically known as migration. People put all the different means of transportation into use in the process of migration. The roads are clogged with retinue of vehicles, the railways and airports are also crowded with people being taken from place to place. The deserts are also marked with footsteps of those resorting to this alternative as a way to embark also on this migration. "The movement of peoples has become a familiar feature of contemporary life, perhaps without historical precedent at such a level of magnitude, until the world seems to be filled up with traffic of all kinds bound in every direction at once."[1]

It is a well known fact that human beings are ever on the move. They not only move about or from place to place, they also move with their luggage. In fact, one can not set out on a journey without an almost

---

[1] Parsons, S. F., (Ed), *Studies in Christian Ethics*, 19.1, London: Sage Publications, 2006, p. 6.

unconscious anticipation of meeting others on the way and countless numbers of peoples are trying to get to someplace.

The migration of peoples can be categorized into two forms, thus: voluntary and forced migration. The method of locomotion of the particular individual sometimes defines the category of such movement. Those forced to migrate deserve a lot of attention. They are those individuals who leave or are driven from what they know as home and who may, thereby, become displaced.[2] Often their movements away are unheeded as many cling to the bottom of already moving trains, or are found frozen in the wheels of aircraft, or crawling along tunnels in the dark or are parked like sardines in the ship. Many of these forced migrants, due to their mediocrity, deal with disreputable agents, thus risking further their already dangerous and distressing lives. Many end up in this way infamously, while others end up honourably. But as people take leave of a place, they meet on their way out others who are entering. Whatever may be the reason, a poor economy attracts as many to come as it drives into exile. Disasters blow out the devastated and (bring) in those willing to help.[3] The tracks and exhaustion of migrating people are everywhere.

The paradox of migration brings the issues of nationality to question when it transverses the boundaries of a given nation. This is the concern of immigration policies. When an international movement is legal,[4] then a valid stipulated visa should be presented otherwise the migrants are considered to be illegal. This attitude, in as much as it is plausible, has its own flaws and short sightedness. The corrections of such short sightedness, and the enlightenment and creation of awareness of the sufferings of the so called illegal migrants and other migrants as a whole is the aim of this work.

---

[2] Cf. Ibid., p. 7.

[3] Cf. Parson, S.F., op. cit. p. 6. Brackets mine.

[4] This refers to the adherence to the given immigration regulations of a country.

Without prejudice to those migrants with valid visas, all those who move into a new country other than their original ones are categorized as strangers. This is the first division which encompasses all migrants within one nomenclature – expatriate. Then, for those without a valid visa, the next governmental alternative for them is deportation, except if they get the status of Asylum or Refugee, or are on the process of getting it. "They are ones who live beyond the bounds, appearing as strangers among others, and whose search for a place that will accept and accommodate them defines them as sojourners temporarily staying here."[5] In any case, there is always a growing tension between the migrants who found themselves overtly or covertly within the confines of a nation, and those who are citizens of such a nation.

Our main area of concern is the migrant Africans who are in Europe. Though there are a lot of them who are legally settled, there are lots more who are not. Many are seeking to be recognized as asylums and others as refugees. Each group has found itself battling with the tenets of law whose code of understanding and practise revolve around the walls and checkpoints erected by groups of people to preserve themselves. There is no problem in doing that, especially when the aim is to preserve the legacy of the nation. In this work, we shall try and have an overview of the situation and attempt an appraisal of it. Migration, asylum and refugee seeking in the last few decades have become a perennial problem. The people have always been met with consternation, though caused sometimes, by themselves through their attitudes. In each of these, the manner of their comportment with others is of primary concern. That notwithstanding, we are called upon to deal with one another out of respect and care as creatures of God, and to find the roots of friendship that may counteract fear and rejection and thwart the smooth running of human life. It is to be noted that those who are involved in this movement are human beings, and as such whatever should charac-

---

[5] Parson, S.F., Ibid, p. 7.

terise the conduct of inter-subjective relations with them should centre on love, tolerance, understanding and care. Human beings should be seen, considered, and treated as human beings and not as "things" thrown off as by-products of the now limitless mad movement in the world called migration.

This research work is divided into five chapters. In the first chapter, we tried to give a working definition and explication of the important key terms in our work, thus: Migration, Asylum seekers, and Refugees. The definitions attempted in this chapter are only an approach to the subjects based on our restricted ambience of research. They are defined with the view of the nature of their different claims in mind. As a result of that these claims help in no small measure in our subjecting the central political issues concerning the issue of migration, asylum and refugee seeking to ethical scrutiny. In this chapter, we tried to cite the definitions and understanding of the United Nations Organisation (UNO) on the subject. The Universal Declaration of Human Right was used as a paradigm.

We proceeded next into chapter two where we examined the situation as it is in Africa. This is to give us a clear and general picture of the continent from which these Euro-African migrants originated. It is pertinent to note that the picture of the African society as can be seen here is not in detail. Only those aspects which are necessary for our purpose here were researched into with the aim of projecting those aspects latter as the part of the reasons why the migrants embark on the journey. Besides, we did not cover the whole of the African society in this research work. That would not only be impossible, but also unnecessary in a research work of this nature. Thus we limited our ambience to the Nigerian society which is the most populated multi-ethnic nation in Africa.

Having made an exposition of the African society in a general, though non-detailed form, we then turned to the concrete reasons that necessitate the movement of people into Europe as refugees or asylum seekers. This was our aim in chapter three. Following the dictates of the human rights and the natural instinct in man, there were justifications for the migration of the people. A justification which is strengthened by the fact that the right to life is inalienable and it belongs to man as man. We researched into the argument in favour of preservation of life and when it is endangered the right to protect it. Hunger and persecution can be a threat to life and when these are imminent the best option will be to 'move'. This is the situation in most of the African countries. With this establishment, we pushed for some practical realities in the reception and acceptance of the migrants as citizens of one human society. With the arguments of the church and some of the social encyclicals dealing with the topic, we tackled this issue in chapter four of this research work.

Chapter five ends the research with a critical evaluation and a general appraisal of the situation. In this final section of the work, we tried to bring together the ethical, practical and social lessons of the previous chapters in order to arrive at some critical appraisal of the work.

Finally, it is important to note that the topic of this research is a current issue in the world's politics and socio-economic order. The church has a role to play in this direction and as a watch dog for morality; she intervenes with some ideal standards as a measure of control for the excesses of the world's political issues, especially issues that concern human beings.

As a broad area and a current issue of the 21st century, we cannot claim to have covered the area summarily. But the aim of the whole research is to present the unjustifiable nature of any attempt aimed at annihilation of migration on bases not connected with the consideration of common good, and to decry the inhuman treatment of those migrants who on account of the situations in their home countries are made to become citizens of no country. These migrants live in between two worlds: the world out of which they came and into which it is not safe for them to enter; and the world into which they want to enter but which will not let them in.

What we have attempted to do in this work is to analyse the challenges facing the whole world polity with regard to the ethically ideal response to the problems of refugees and asylum seekers all over the world. Drawing from the practical experiences of different nations and the relevance of the church's teachings on this area, we tried to make a response in a modest way to this phenomenon.

Methodological Approach

The method used in this work is mainly literature review based on the discussion on the issue of migration as presented in some works already done on the topic. The analytical aspect of the work focuses on those factors, as can be deduced from concrete narrations, which make people susceptible to migrate away from their home country. The concept of migration (including illegal migration) and the responses of the international bodies and the Catholic Church to problems caused by it are analysed and discussed. To form a solid base for the presentation of the strategies for the intervention of the stakeholders in fighting the problems, the formal juridical explanations where given to the terms migration, asylum seekers and refugees. The main focus in the work is Nigeria and the Nigerian migrants to Europe although, where necessary, references are made to other countries and non-Nigerian migrants.

1

BASIC EXPLANATIONS AND UNDERSTANDING

1.1 Remarks

For a good scholarship, we have to attempt to clarify and explain the main terms that run across the whole of this research work. This will present the ambience from which this work views the attendant problems to the public more vividly. It is to be noted that in any definition of terms such as the ones used in this work, there are often some lapses which are noticed in the definition, and this work is no exception. The understanding of who a migrant is will be based on our understanding of what migration is. And the understanding of an asylum seeker and a refugee will be based on our understanding of the scope of the status of both.

1.2 Migrants

This is a term used to designate those persons who move from one place to the other for a purpose. This movement is classically referred to as migration. Migration can be internal or external (international). It can also be permanent or temporal: "Migration generally involves a permanent, semi permanent or temporary change of residence. But the causes of migration have remained one of the focal issues in migration studies."[6] In defining human migration, Encyclopaedia Britannica excludes "such movements as nomadism, migrant labour, commuting, and tourism, all of which are transitory in nature."[7] I agree with this exclusion since in our work here, we are dealing with migrants as permanent residents in the new found location. That is, those who move from their countries of origin to another one for whatever reason, and are not willing to go back either at all, or only for visit if need be. This is distinguished from internal movements of individuals and families from one part of the country to the other or from the rural area to the urban. Whether internal or external (international), migration can be voluntary or forced.

In the consideration of migration as being either voluntary or forced, Matthew Gibney (2004) used the terms 'pull' and 'push' to distinguish the determining factors; "the traditional way of distinguishing between economic migrants and refugees has been by reference to the 'push' and 'pull' factors that motivate international migration. Put simply, 'push' factors are generally conceived of as negative influences that encourage people to emigrate from a country, such as political instability, a low standard of living, civil war, etc. 'Pull' factors, on the other hand, are positive influences that draw immigrants to a particular state such as a high standard of living, democratic political institutions, excess demand for labour, etc."[8] This corresponds to the explanation and classification of causes of migration as quoted by Mgbeafulu (2003);

> "In his 'A Theory of Migration' Lee identified such factors as the pull and push factors. The former is associated with attractions of destination area while the latter is associated with those

---

[6] Mgbeafulu, M.C., *Migration and the Economy*, New York: iUniverse, Inc., 2003, p. 29.

[7] Encyclopaedia Britannica, 15th edition, U.S.A: Encyclopaedia Britannica, Inc., 2002, Vol. 6, p. 136.

[8] Gibney, M. J., *The Ethics and Politics of Asylum*, New York: Cambridge University Press, 2004, p. 11.

intervening or impulsive factors that pushed one to move out of his ancestral home."[9]

Migration is a process of humanity and belongs to the action of man. Robert Winder (2005) puts it in another way; "True, I wasn't an immigrant. But I soon saw that we are all immigrants: it simply depends how far back you go."[10] Most of the citizens of a given nation are immigrants. It is the most ancient action in the history of humanity against poverty and threatening situation. People tend to move when the situation is not more favourable.

The dominant trend in migration in the 20th and 21st centuries has been the migration from Africa to Europe. The number of African migrants in the late 20th century and the 21st century cannot be compared with the number in any other century in the history of Africa. This number has continued to grow because of the situations which are not in a way favourable for a decent living. Due to the nature of the conditions and situations of the migrants, grave difficulties are encountered by different nations in the arduous task of identifying an economic migrant and an asylum seeker. But a clear distinction can be made of the two by using the simple analogy made by Gibney (2004): "If economic migrants are refused entry, they are forced to remain in a situation of poverty; if (asylum seekers) are turned away, their very lives may well be on the line."[11]

1.3 Asylum Seekers

It is to be noted that sometimes it is difficult to distinguish between asylum seekers and refugees since all are strangers and are weak and dependent on the host country for their survival and support. Matthew

---

[9] Mbeafulu, M.C., Op.cit., p. 30.

[10] Winder, R., *Bloody Foreigners*, Great Britain: Little, Brown, 2005, p. x.

[11] Ibid, p. 12. Brackets mine.

Gibney (2004) puts it thus: "The asylum applicant makes exactly the same moral claim for entrance as the refugee: allow me to enter for if you do not I will be persecuted or placed in life-threatening danger."[12] However, a line of thin difference cuts across the two. When we hear of the word 'asylum' the thought of 'a place of shelter, safety or protection' immediately comes to the mind. An asylum seeker can be a refugee, but the reverse may not be the case. In trying to define who an asylum seeker is, the Britannica Americana recognizes that "the protection of the individual migrating on basis of security first of all begins with asylum."[13] In this case, the individual migrant's right to asylum is a concomitant to the right to life.

Migration, as we saw earlier, can be forced as well as voluntary. A forced migration can be caused naturally by disasters or by humans (e.g. governments), and in either case; one responds to the natural basic instinct in human beings, that is, the preservation of life. "Migration usually involves people who have been expelled by government during war or other political upheavals."[14] These people run to other countries to seek for protection against the threats to their lives. This gives them the status of asylum. Asylum is the name used to designate the status of a migrant who wishes to remain in a country other than his own on reasons of safety.

As stated above, asylum means a place of refuge, shelter or protection. The term is also used "…to denote the protection afforded by such a refuge and the right to grant such a refuge."[15] The right to demand for an asylum status and to receive it does not fall directly within the basic fundamental human right as decorated by the United Nations. It is only

---

[12] Ibid. p. 9.

[13] Encyclopaedia Americana, International Edition, Canada: Grolier Limited, 1976, Vol. 9, p. 183.

[14] Encyclopaedia Britannica, Op. cit., p. 137.

[15] Encyclopaedia Americana, Op. cit., Vol.2, p. 595.

implied. The right to grant or not to grant it is solely that of the host country. "The person for whom asylum is established has no legal right to demand it, while the sheltering state, which has the legal right to grant asylum, is under no obligation to give it."[16] Thus this definition presents asylum as a specific right of the state and not that of the individual.

There are three basic classical categories of asylum: Territorial, extraterritorial, and neutral asylum. Territorial asylum is usually granted within the territorial boundary of the country granting it. This is most of the time granted to people fleeing their countries of origin on reasons of political offences, for instance, treason. Most of the people seeking for asylum fall within this category. Extraterritorial asylum is more of a strategic structural action than a simple protection against a physical threat to one's life or an unjust aggressor.[17] This refers to "...asylum granted in legations, consulates, and warships and merchant vessels in foreign territory. It is therefore granted within the territory of the state from which protection is sought."[18] Sometimes, this is granted to individuals in the compound of another embassy within the country that is threatening the individual. This is also known as diplomatic asylum. Neutral asylum is usually a practice done during war. "...used by a state neutral in time of war, which is considered to have the right to offer asylum within its territory to troops of belligerent states."[19]

However, the opportunity to seek for asylum is open for everyone who faces persecution and a threat to his or her life. "Every one has the right to seek and to enjoy in other countries asylum from persecution."[20] In the typical African traditional setting, asylum is also granted in places of refuge, for example, shrines and some designated forests; one can not

---

[16] Encyclopaedia Britannica, Op. cit., Vol.1, p. 659.

[17] Ibid.

[18] Ibid.

[19] Ibid.

[20] See article 14, Universal Declaration of Human Rights, 1948.

be forcibly removed or violently touched without the action being considered as a sacrilege when one is in this place. "Special taboos and rules prevented the profanation of sanctuaries. It was because of this special sacred quality and the protection that it afforded that the sanctuary became a place of asylum."[21] The issue of asylum seeking is an international community issue and the latter assists the states where the burden of asylum weighs the economy down. However, granting asylum to the desperate men and women is a response of a nation to meet their needs as refugees. And what the refugee needs is the security of the new nation in which he or she now resides.

1.4 Refugees

According to the definition of Encyclopaedia Britannica, a refugee is "any uprooted, homeless, involuntary migrant who has crossed a frontier and no longer possesses the protection of his former government."[22] This definition is in line with the real situation and state of those migrants who have or are seeking to be recognized as refugees. The main aspect to be focused on in the understanding and treatment of a refugee is that a potential refugee is without security and thus, seeks for one; that the refugee or one seeking for such a status still faces a deteriorating situation is due to the world's growing insensitivity to human problems and sufferings. However, we may not rule out the fact that the tremendous growth in the number of people seeking the status of refugees also contributes to the negligence of the refugees.

Owing to the complexity of the refugee situations and the emergency that goes with it, the definition can be said to be broadened. In 1951, the United Nations Convention regarded and concluded that a refugee is anyone who

---

[21] Encyclopaedia Britannica, Op.cit, Vol. 10, p. 405.

[22] Ibid. Vol.9, p. 998.

> "...owing to well founded fear of being persecuted for reasons of race, religion, nationality, membership of a particular social group or political opinion, is outside the country of his nationality and is unable or, owing to such fear, is unwilling to avail himself of the protection of that country; or who, not having a nationality and being outside the country of his former habitual residence as a result of such events, is unable to return to it."[23]

There are so many definitions and views on what should constitute the actual understanding of refugee. The one used most frequently is the one cited above as coming from the UN 1951 convention and it is the one which most liberal democratic nation have adopted. There is a little lack in the definition of a refugee given by the UN because its emphasis on 'persecution' excludes all those who, due to other prevailing factors that tantamount to threats to their lives, are forced to flee their countries. For example,

> "under the somewhat dubious interpretation of the Refugee Convention recently used by France and Germany, women who have fled the oppressive structures of the Taliban, Iraqis displaced by the US and British war to disarm Saddam Hussein, in addition to Zairians escaping the deadly Ebola virus, may not be considered refugees. For these groups are not on the move because they have been persecuted, in the sense that their state has deliberately targeted them for ill-treatment."[24]

Perhaps owing to the inadequacy of the UN definition in terms of covering all or most of the factors that may lead one to seeking the status of a refugee, the Organization of African Unity (OAU) offered a supplementary definition of a refugee to the universal one supplied by the UN. The spectrum of the definition covers "every person who, owing to external aggression, occupation, foreign domination or events

---

[23] Encyclopaedia Americana, Op cit., vol. 9, p. 182.

[24] Gibney, M.J., Op.cit., p. 7.

seriously disturbing public order in either part or the whole of his country of origin or nationality, is compelled to leave his place of habitual residence in order to seek refuge in another place outside his country of nationality.[25]

From the above definitions of a refugee, it is to be noted that one who enjoys a protection or receives one from a particular country cannot seek for another on the platform of refugee situations. In as much as most countries recognize and accept dual nationalities, such duality is not possible in the case of seeking for a refugee status. As a refugee, one enjoys an international protection, a privilege enjoyed by one as a substitute for the national protection one looses when one's link with the country of origin is severed. This helps to protect the interest of the individual and to assure the respect of one's basic fundamental human rights.

According to Hannah Arendt in her book on 'the origin of Totalitarianism' she sees the refugees from the point of view of the treatments melted out to them. This informed her working definition of them as "...people who had indeed lost all other qualities and specific relationships-except that they were still human."[26]

Refugee movements are caused by many factors ranging from man-made causes e.g. crisis, war, and intolerance, to natural causes, e.g. natural catastrophe and outbreak of diseases. These movements can also be within the country, that is, internally, or outside the country, that is, externally. The internally displaced persons, though they face a considerable level of intimidations and oppressions among their hosts, are

---

[25] Ibid. see also Schacknove, A., 'Who is a Refugee?' *Ethics* 95, 2:274-84. Mark Gibney (ed.), *Open Borders? Closed Societies?: The Ethical and Political Issues*, Westport: Greenwood Press, 1988.

[26] Arendt, H. *The Origin of Totalitarianism*. New York: Harcourt Brace Jovanovich, 1979, p. 229.

nevertheless not to be compared with their counterparts who are in foreign lands.

In relation to the refugees, the 1951 convention accords the refugee the right to enjoy the same favourable treatments as the other citizens in many ways.

> "Refugees are to enjoy treatment as favourable as possible, and no less favourable than that accorded to aliens in general with regard to the acquisition of movable or immovable property and other related rights, activity on a self employed basis... the establishment of commercial and industrial companies...and access to higher education."[27]

In understanding of the meaning of a refugee and, for our interest in this research work, it is very pertinent to emphasise that among all the privileges, a refugee should enjoy to protect his or her basic right, the highest and the most valuable of them all is the right to stay away from the impending danger to his or her life, especially from the place where this danger resides. "A key provision of the convention protects refugees from expulsion or return to a country where their life or freedom would be threatened."[28]

1.5 Universal Declaration of Human Rights

Human rights could be said to be those rights of man endowed to him by nature and which cannot be denied or removed from him without being considered as an infringement. These rights are inalienable. According to the United Nations Bill of Human Rights, "All human beings are born free and equal in dignity and rights. They are endowed with reason and conscience and should act towards one another in a spirit of

---

[27] Ibid.

[28] Ibid.

brotherhood."[29] The fact that man has a fundamental right is a gift to him from nature and not a privilege bestowed on him by any human postulations. In fact, it could be positively argued that Human Rights as declared by the United nations General Assembly of 1948 is only a subtle way of emphasising the natural rights which God gave to man.

Since the core of this research will be based on the fundamental human rights of the individuals who suffer due to their states, and also to a greater extent, to that of the countries into which the migrants move, we have to state the universal Declaration of Human Rights as adopted by the United nations General Assembly in Paris in full.

Article 1

All human beings are born free and equal in dignity and rights. They are endowed with reason and conscience and should act towards one another in a spirit of brotherhood.

Article 2

Everyone is entitled to all the rights and freedoms set forth in this Declaration, without distinction of any kind, such as race, colour, sex, language, religion, political or other opinion, national or social origin, property, birth or other status. Furthermore, no distinction shall be made on the basis of the political, jurisdictional or international status of the country or territory to which a person belongs, whether it is independent, trust, non-self-governing or under any other limitation of sovereignty.

Article 3

Everyone has the right to life, liberty and security of person.

---

[29] Universal Declaration of Human Rights (art.1), United Nations General Assembly Resolution, 217 A (111), 10th December, 1948, see http://www.unhchr.ch/html/menu6. 29.03.2007. Henceforth UNDHR.

Article 4

No one shall be held in slavery or servitude; slavery and the slave trade shall be prohibited in all their forms.

Article 5

No one shall be subjected to torture or to cruel, inhuman or degrading treatment or punishment.

Article 6

Everyone has the right to recognition everywhere as a person before the law.

Article 7

All are equal before the law and are entitled without any discrimination to equal protection of the law. All are entitled to equal protection against any discrimination in violation of this Declaration and against any incitement to such discrimination.

Article 8

Everyone has the right to an effective remedy by the competent national tribunals for acts violating the fundamental rights granted him by the constitution or by law.

Article 9

No one shall be subjected to arbitrary arrest, detention or exile.

Article 10

Everyone is entitled in full equality to a fair and public hearing by an independent and impartial tribunal, in the determination of his rights and obligations and of any criminal charge against him.

Article 11

- Everyone charged with a penal offence has the right to be presumed innocent until proved guilty according to law in a public trial at which he has had all the guarantees necessary for his defence.
- No one shall be held guilty of any penal offence on account of any act or omission which did not constitute a penal offence, under national or international law, at the time when it was committed. Nor shall a heavier penalty be imposed than the one that was applicable at the time the penal offence was committed.

Article 12

No one shall be subjected to arbitrary interference with his privacy, family, home or correspondence, nor to attacks upon his honour and reputation. Everyone has the right to the protection of the law against such interference or attacks.

Article 13

- Everyone has the right to freedom of movement and residence within the borders of each state.
- Everyone has the right to leave any country, including his own, and to return to his country.

Article 14

- Everyone has the right to seek and to enjoy in other countries asylum from persecution.
- This right may not be invoked in the case of prosecutions genuinely arising from non-political crimes or from acts contrary to the purposes and principles of the United Nations.

Article 15

- Everyone has the right to a nationality.

- No one shall be arbitrarily deprived of his nationality nor denied the right to change his nationality.

Article 16

- Men and women of full age, without any limitation due to race, nationality or religion, have the right to marry and to found a family. They are entitled to equal rights as to marriage, during marriage and at its dissolution.
- Marriage shall be entered into only with the free and full consent of the intending spouses.
- The family is the natural and fundamental group unit of society and is entitled to protection by society and the State.

Article 17

- Everyone has the right to own property alone as well as in association with others.
- No one shall be arbitrarily deprived of his property.

Article 18

Everyone has the right to freedom of thought, conscience and religion; this right includes freedom to change his religion or belief, and freedom, either alone or in community with others and in public or private, to manifest his religion or belief in teaching, practice, worship and observance.

Article 19

Everyone has the right to freedom of opinion and expression; this right includes freedom to hold opinions without interference and to seek, receive and impart information and ideas through any media and regardless of frontiers.

Article 20

- Everyone has the right to freedom of peaceful assembly and association.
- No one may be compelled to belong to an association.

Article 21

- Everyone has the right to take part in the government of his country, directly or through freely chosen representatives.
- Everyone has the right of equal access to public service in his country.
- The will of the people shall be the basis of the authority of government; this will shall be expressed in periodic and genuine elections which shall be by universal and equal suffrage and shall be held by secret vote or by equivalent free voting procedures.

Article 22

Everyone, as a member of society, has the right to social security and is entitled to realization, through national effort and international co-operation and in accordance with the organization and resources of each State, of the economic, social and cultural rights indispensable for his dignity and the free development of his personality.

Article 23

- Everyone has the right to work, to free choice of employment, to just and favourable conditions of work and to protection against unemployment.
- Everyone, without any discrimination, has the right to equal pay for equal work.
- Everyone who works has the right to just and favourable remuneration ensuring for himself and his family an existence worthy of human dignity, and supplemented, if necessary, by other means of social protection.

- Everyone has the right to form and to join trade unions for the protection of his interests.

Article 24

Everyone has the right to rest and leisure, including reasonable limitation of working hours and periodic holidays with pay.

Article 25

- Everyone has the right to a standard of living adequate for the health and well-being of himself and of his family, including food, clothing, and housing and medical care and necessary social services, and the right to security in the event of unemployment, sickness, disability, widowhood, old age or other lack of livelihood in circumstances beyond his control.
- Motherhood and childhood are entitled to special care and assistance. All children, whether born in or out of wedlock, shall enjoy the same social protection.

Article 26

- Everyone has the right to education. Education shall be free, at least in the elementary and fundamental stages. Elementary education shall be compulsory. Technical and professional education shall be made generally available and higher education shall be equally accessible to all on the basis of merit.
- Education shall be directed to the full development of the human personality and to the strengthening of respect for human rights and fundamental freedoms. It shall promote understanding, tolerance and friendship among all nations, racial or religious groups, and shall further the activities of the United Nations for the maintenance of peace.
- Parents have a prior right to choose the kind of education that shall be given to their children.

Article 27

- Everyone has the right freely to participate in the cultural life of the community, to enjoy the arts and to share in scientific advancement and its benefits.
- Everyone has the right to the protection of the moral and material interests resulting from any scientific, literary or artistic production of which he is the author.

Article 28

Everyone is entitled to a social and international order in which the rights and freedoms set forth in this Declaration can be fully realized.

Article 29

- Everyone has duties to the community in which alone the free and full development of his personality is possible.
- In the exercise of his rights and freedoms, everyone shall be subject only to such limitations as are determined by law solely for the purpose of securing due recognition and respect for the rights and freedoms of others and of meeting the just requirements of morality, public order and the general welfare in a democratic society.
- These rights and freedoms may in no case be exercised contrary to the purposes and principles of the United Nations.

Article 30

Nothing in this Declaration may be interpreted as implying for any State, group or person any right to engage in any activity or to perform any act aimed at the destruction of any of the rights and freedoms set forth herein.

This United Nation Declaration of Human Right (UNDHR) has received some praises and like every other human enterprise, it has also witnessed some criticisms. The predominantly Muslim nations have criticised it and accused it of not taking into account the Islamic laws. They regard it as being a by-product of the modernized Judaeo-Christian tradition as contained in the present Christian Bible.

In reaction to the UNDHR, the Cairo Declaration of Human rights was adopted by 45 foreign Ministers of the Organisation of the Islamic Conference on August 5, 1990 as guidance for their states in issues concerning human rights. This declaration states that: "There shall be no crime or punishment except as provided for in the sharia."[30] In their view and recommendations, the UNDHR should be adhered to only in so far as it corresponds to the dictates of the sharia laws. It therefore implies that whatever is in the UNDHR that does not correspond with the sharia Law may be viewed with consternation.

---

[30] Cairo Declaration of Human Rights, August 5, 1990, Art. 19(D), see also http://www.religlaw.org/interdocs/docs/cairohrislam1990.htm. 5.04.2007

2

THE AFRICAN CONTINENT: PEOPLE AND SITUATION

2.1 Origin and Nature of the People

Like every thing on earth, the continent of Africa has an origin. But like most of the things on earth, the origin of Africa as a continent is not quite clear. The reason for this difficulty in arriving with certainty at the precise origin of Africa is because the continent is ancient and there are little or no original records of ancient events as we have it today. But for the sake of scholarship, certain presumptions have been made as to the origin of Africa.

According to the statistics of Encyclopaedia Britannica, Africa is

> "... the second largest continent, after Asia, covering about one fifth of the total land surface of the Earth. The continent is bounded on the west by the Atlantic ocean, on the north by the Mediterranean sea, on the east by the Red sea and the Indian ocean, and on the south by the mingling waters of the Atlantic and Indian oceans."[31]

The word 'Africa' cannot be identified with any of the more than 1000 languages that are being spoken all over Africa, among the more than 730 million people and in the 50 countries that dot the map of the continent of Africa. "Africa is a common name people used to designate

---

[31] Encyclopaedia Britannica, Op.cit., Vol.1, p. 131.

the continent that harbours so many countries, over 720 million people and over 1000 languages. The name has been credited to a Berber origin."[32]

Since the name 'Africa' has a relationship of implication with the Latin word 'aprica' and the Greek word 'aphrike,' the two words meaning : 'sunny,' and 'without cold' respectively, the morphology of the word 'Africa' is not too far from being an outcome of a Greco-Roman invention.

"Many others have traced the name 'Africa' to Greco-Roman ancestry [...]. The Romans referred to their colonial province in the present day Tunisia as 'Africa' possibly because the name came from the Latin or Greek word for that region or its people…."[33] But there are further speculations that the geographical location of the continent with the consequent climatic condition informed the minds of the early users of the name Africa to designate this part of the world as such. In using the name Africa,

> "…it is credible to see a connection from Latin (Africa=sunny) and Greek (Aphrike=not cold). The Romans were being inspired to the name from some of the first people they met on the continent: The Afris, which were a Berber tribe in the Carthage area. Egypt was already a known territory, but further south it was an unknown land. Somewhere round 2000 years ago "Ethiopia" seems to have been used to describe the land found south of Sahara, but Europeans later used "Africa" to describe the entire continent."[34]

Before the advent of the white explorers to Africa, there were no categorized boundaries. The existence of boundaries was an invention of

---

[32] Mazrui, A., quoted in Ilo S.C., *The Face of Africa, Looking beyond the Shadows*, U.S.A: Author House UK, 2006, p. 7.

[33] Ibid.

[34] http://crawfurd.dk/africa/woed.htm. 5.04.2007.

the European colonial masters. Actually, in order to understand the history of Africa very well one needs to make references to the historical documentations of the colonial exploitations.

> "Obviously the colonial exploitation had given the Africans some kind of a common history. But long before any white man set foot in Africa, the tribes and people had already been mixed together and switched homelands several times. Obviously, there are similarities between tribes and people in Africa."[35]

African history, although not a fixed concluded fact, is peculiar. Its peculiarity is because of the scientific suggestions that the continent is a very important point of departure in the understanding of the history of humanity. This has a scientific perspective because "modern science recognizes Africa as the cradle of humankind."[36]

Science goes by method of deduction and analysis of fact and figures to arrive at a conclusion. Studies conducted and the results arrived at show Africa as an ancient continent.

> "The Africa continent essentially consists of five ancient Precambrian crotons (kaapvall, Zimbabwe, Tanzania, Congo an West Africa) that were formed between about 3.6 and 2.0 billion years ago and that basically have been tectonically stable since that time...."[37]

The oldest rocks known on earth are found in the greenstone terrains of Zimbabwe and Congo crotons.[38] By inference, one can conclude that Africa dates very back in historical time. According to Archaeological

---

[35] Ibid.

[36] The New partnership for Africa's Development, no. 14, a draft by the Justice and peace Department of the South African Catholic Bishop's Conference, 2002.

[37] Africa, 'Geologic History', in Encyclopaedia Britannica, 2005 Ultimate Reference Suite (DVD).

[38] See Ibid.

findings, human beings have lived in the continent of Africa some millions of years ago.

> "Archaeological evidence indicates that the continent (of Africa) has been inhabited by humans and their hominid forebears for some 4,000,000, years or more. Anatomically, modern humans are believed to have appeared about 100,000 years ago in the eastern region of sub-Saharan Africa. Somewhat later these early humans spread...to the rest of the world."[39]

This scientific rendition echoes the statement that "...humans have lived in Africa far longer than anywhere else."[40]

The majority of Africans are black in colour, although there are a considerable number who are white. Being an African does not necessarily mean that one is a black person. There are over a thousand individual tribes, languages, social and cultural diversities in the continent which account for the complexity of the continent. There is a mixture of black, Caucasian, Asian and Indian races. There is also the Arab race in Africa. "Besides the ethnic diversity of Africa, the continent is also made up of European and Asian races numbering several millions who have settled and intermarried with African native tribes."[41] The colour difference is due to the many climatic variables and other morphological features present in the continent. The weather is also very hot most of the times of the year than in any other part of the earth.

Although the death rate in Africa is on the high side, the birth rate is also high and that accounts for the continent's huge population which is the fastest growing population in the world. Africa constitutes about 10% of the world's population. This does not match adequately with the size of the continent as the second largest continent, being next to Asia

---

[39] Africa, 'The people', Ibid.

[40] Diamond, J, et al, *The Fates of Human Societies*, New York: W.W. Norton and Company, 1999, p. 377.

[41] Ilo, S. C., Op.cit., p. 8.

which is the largest. In almost all the countries in Africa, the population is made up of more people between the age of 15 and 25 years. Some parts of Africa have been occupied since the evolution of humanity while some parts, especially the desert areas appear not to be or ever to have been occupied at all.

2.2 African Family System and Community

The family is the unity and basis of an African community. To understand the structural set-up of the African community, a reference must be made to the system of family that exists in the African society. The family is the source of strength for the whole community and the size of the family determines a lot in the life of that family in particular and the strength of the community in general. The information given in this work is based on what obtains in a typical African family and society that is not adulterated by the influx of the western mentality and culture. Usually a family set-up is determined by its economic strength which, in turn, is determined by the number of persons in it. "The forms of the family found in Africa are consistent with the forms of economic production."[42] Unlike what obtains in the developed world, in Africa, the family is not only the immediate family members as a group of persons in one house. The family extends to include a lot of direct siblings and relations to a certain generation. "Throughout most of the rural areas, the typical domestic group is the joint or extended family consisting of several generations of kin and their spouses, the whole being under the authority of the senior male."[43] There is no exact number of persons that should be in a family. This is no rule, but usually a typical African couple has about seven children in addition to the extended

---

[42] Africa, 'Domestic Groupings', Encyclopaedia Britannica, 2005 Ultimate Reference, Op. cit.
[43] Ibid.

families which include the family lineage up to the fourth or the fifth generation.

> "The size of the group varies, but it typically consists of three to five generations of kin. It provides a stable and long-lasting domestic unit able to work as a single cooperative group, to defend itself against others, and to care for all of its members throughout their life times."[44]

This extension of the family make-up and the life pattern has influenced to a very great extent, the social life of the African people. Because the family is large, the community derives its worth and pattern of life from the family system. There is the practise of welcoming the so-called strangers and visitors. But in actual fact, in the African community setup, there is no stranger. What obtains is the idea of neighbour and enemy. Everyone is regarded as a neighbour and treated as such; the enemy is seen as a stranger.

2.2.1 Ancestors

In the African society, those individuals who have lived the traditions of the land to the fullest and in accordance with the standard of conduct are regarded as ancestors. "One can see them as human models of correct behaviour."[45] The descendants are expected to follow in the footsteps of these ancestors to ensure continuity. Though they are dead, they are considered as still living and are regularly invoked by the living in terms of needs. Not all the ancestors are invoked, but only those of them who led a good and exemplary life. The ancestors are not vindictive. They act with honour. However, they can punish those who deviate from the norm or the acceptable standard code of conduct as a warning that such behaviours and deviations are improper.

---

[44] Ibid.

[45] Anigbo, O.A.C., *Igbo Elite and Western Europe*, Onitsha Nigeria, Africana-Fep Publishers,1992, p. 32.

The living members of the African society do not fear the ancestors as long as they act accordingly. The hope of being with the ancestor is the greatest desire of an African. "The desire for the Igbo[46] is to be with his ancestors."[47] These ancestors who are dead are sometimes worshipped. In some parts of Africa, they are venerated and considered as part of the family. The spirits of the ancestors are believed to have the powers to intervene in the affairs of the family and can bring about many changes in the lives of the living, both for good as in a reward, and for bad as in a punishment. "They are called as witnesses and judges in cases of unjust treatment of the poor and down trodden. They are the hope of the oppressed."[48]

Usually, an ancestor is remote in the line of family decent. In the remote placement of the family lineage stands the ancestor as one from whom the family descended.

2.2.2 Extended Family System

It is generally accepted that the family is the fundamental unit of every society. Love and tenderness, security and social stability, and other basic necessities of life and health are made available at the beginning of the life of the individual through family set up. This is in consonance with what John Lawson Degbey, director Africa Rights of the Child Foundation said. For him, the family

> "is a cohesive unit which ideally provides economic (land for farming etc) social and psychological security to all its members. It defines social and moral norms and safeguards material and

---

[46] This is a tribe found in the eastern part of Nigeria in West Africa.

[47] Jordan, J. P. *Bishop Shanahan of Southern Nigeria*. Dublin: Clonmore & Reynolds, 1949 quoted in Anigbo, O.A.C., Ibid., p. 32.

[48] Ndiokwere, N.I., *Search for Greener Pastures: Igbo and African Experience*, USA: Morris Publishing, 1998, p. 156.

spiritual customs and traditions as well as providing a variety of role models in preparing the way for adulthood."[49]

In the African society, this extends even to a very important family structure known as the extended family system.

In the traditional, rural African societies, the extended family includes not only the immediate family members comprising the man and his wife and their children, but also, "…cousins, uncles and aunts living in a compound or close to one another form the family."[50] A basic definition of the extended family system is somehow difficult to arrive at in the general African society, but the important fact is that, anyhow the system is defined; it must include the basic structures that make up the extended family in order to be an authentic definition. As we have attempted to state above, it must include the family members beyond the man and his wife and/or children. Thus, the extended family is the more important social structure in the African society as it forms the stronghold upon which the entire society relies. That the family circle in Africa extends far beyond the tight location of the immediate family of a man and his household provides the basis for human respect and honour. "People respect and have affection for one another. Children are treated with much indulgence and affection. They will go into any house where they have a (relation) and be sure of a welcome. No invitation is needed and no pre-information of such a visit is anticipated."[51] The extended family system is more solid in socio-economic strength. It incorporates more members and makes inter-human relationship more functional. Due to this advantage, it is a source of support to the other.

---

[49] Degbey, J.L., Africa Family Structure, in http://www.jicef.or.jp/wahec/ful217.htm. 21.05.2007.

[50] Ibid., see also Matrilineal Traditional African Family, http://www.bridgewater.edu/~mtembo/africantraditionalfamily,htm.21.05.2007.

[51] Anyanwu, S.E.N., *The Igbo Family Life and Cultural Change*, unpublished Thesis, University of Marburg, 1976, p. 168. Brackets mine.

2.2.3 Nuclear Family System

Although the African society is traditionally viewed to be extended in its family structures, when compared with the Western society, in the course of time, some family members wishing to be more independent, though not totally, move away from these structures to form their own small family structures in their own little capacity. This is known as nuclear family. The extended family, also known as the joint family, gives way to the independent nuclear family of husband, wife, and children. There is a difference between the African nuclear family system and the Western nuclear family system. The make-up is the same for both, but the way of life is quite different in both. For the Africans, although the nuclear family is primarily made up of the man and his wife and children, sometimes, another member of the extended family or a relation to either party can also come and live with them.

However, this does not mean that the nuclear family is a replacement of the extended family. The nuclear family system comprises the man, his wife or wives, and his immediate children. In the African society, polygamy is a common practice. This is somehow culturally widespread and seen as the ideal. In some cases, polygamy is a show of wealth. Influential titled men and rulers need marry wives and bear many children to correspond to their level and societal status, and this gives them a mark of high position among other citizens. This status enables the chiefs and rulers to offer hospitality to their subjects.

The nuclear family system started as a result of the economic strength of some individual members of the extended family and their desire to live a somewhat independent life. This independence does not necessarily mean a total break-up of ties with the extended members of the family.

> "During problems and in times of crises, members of the extended family are still expected to help and support (one) another. In

many nuclear families a niece, nephew, aunt, or uncle is also present because he or she needs support."[52]

2.2.4 African Hospitality and Solidarity

African hospitality and solidarity anchors in the African concept of the stranger. This is a cultural heritage which, from whatever angle one views it, is a very important aspect of the African life. This is a pride that is laid open for others to appreciate. The African society is not a closed one; rather, it is an open society. When it comes to issues concerning the stranger and non-residents, the typical African sees in the other the oneness of the human society. Everybody is sure of a welcome at any time and anywhere. The odder the time of the visit, the more attention and consideration one receives. African sense of hospitality and solidarity abhors such practices as social exclusions that are characterized by the unwillingness to show considerations to the other, or the laziness in visiting the other, and inadequate support for the other, especially in terms of need. Such situations are not yet rampant in the African society.

The African sense of hospitality and solidarity and the concept of stranger bring to light the African understanding of neighbourhood. In the African context, a neighbour is every human being who has not proved him/herself as an enemy. This extension of the concept of neighbourhood brings to mind the idea of immigration. This means that Africans are aware of, and are in the practice of migrating ever since the ages. Everywhere they go and in every society they find themselves, they expect to be received though sometimes they do not find people who are ready to receive them, just as they themselves have done either

[52] Family life in Black Communities, in http://family,jrank,org/pages/1613/ South-Africa-Family-Life-in-Black-communities,html. 21.05.2007. Brackets mine.

in their own localities or will definitely do if they are on the hosting side.

The African traditional practice of welcoming is seen, above all, as a sacred duty. According to Nathaniel Ndiokwere,"hospitality is regarded as a sacred institution, through which care, acceptance, and love are extended to the needy...."[53] Although this idea of generosity in the acceptance of the stranger can be detrimental sometimes, the argument on its importance can yield more relevant advantages than otherwise. The socio-economic and cultural advantages are part of the empowerment strategies in Africa. Relationships are established through this practice, ideas are exchanged, and trans-tribal conflicts are prevented. It is however to be noted that in the present-day African society, the destructive effect of colonization in the sense of neighbourhood and solidarity can be felt. This is the case with South Africa where the policies of the apartheid regime fragmented the society into categories that are racial and sectional in structure. This is still, to some extent, the situation in South Africa. Horn Andre of the University of Pretoria, South Africa puts it thus:

> "White society was strictly organised on a territorial basis in which the local school and church played central roles. Black society, confined to the hardship of poorly developed residential townships survived on the basis of a long-established African tradition of *ubuntu,* a form of propinquity and communality that originated in traditional African rural society."[54]

In the course of this research work, random inquiries were made in some states in Nigeria namely: Abuja, Anambra, Enugu, Kano, Lagos,

---

[53] Ndiokwere, N.I., *Search for Greener Pastures: Igbo and African Experience*, USA: Morris Publishing, 1998, p. 74.

[54] Horn, A., *Reflections on the Concept and Conceptualisation of the Urban Neighbourhood in Societies in Transition: The case of Pretoria* (South Africa), in http://www.ff.uni-lj.si/oddleki/geo/publikacihe/dela/file/Dela_ 21/033. 21.05.2007.

and Rivers.[55] The results show that 91% know at least somebody in the far neighbourhood by name and 80% visit at least 3 persons in the far neighbourhood. 80% know at least more than their immediate neighbour by name and more than 90% visit each other in the neighbourhood or has something in common. 90% communicate with each other more regularly, and only about 2% are not at all interested in the other person. Connection with each other is a very interesting aspect of neighbourhood in Africa.

Another interesting aspect of African sense of solidarity is that everyone is free to attend an occasion whether invited or not. Such public functions as weddings, burial ceremonies and allied feasts are very well attended. 70% of the people asked at random are ready to attend a feast, if they know about it, whether they are invited or not. This is understandable because there is no such expression as 'not enough' in the African setting when it comes to the issue of food or entertainment. "Visitors are readily invited to meals and are expected to partake of such meals without qualms. There is always enough provision for the visitor."[56] The quality of the reception may differ depending on the status and nature of the visitor, but the basic needs are provided for and all are welcome, except the known enemy. "This hospitality is not limited to those closely related in the real sense of the word. Hospitality is usually extended to (all)."[57] A further point to emphasize is that the stranger finds shelter in the African society and the host is ready to inconvenience himself to provide for the comfort of the visitor.

An interesting aspect of this random enquiry with regard to our topic here on migration, is that 60% of the people are not ready to migrate far

---

[55] These are some of the states in Nigeria, West Africa, each has over 5 million population. This random inquiry covers the main geo-political regions in the country. See http://www.ngex.com/nigeria/places/states/enugu.htm. 22.09.2007

[56] Ndiokwere, Ibid.

[57] Ndiokwere, Ibid. Brackets mine.

away from their neighbourhood on any account or for what ever reason and 78% are ready to move in search of a better life, but only with regret and a lasting yearning for a return.

In all, the African sense of hospitality and solidarity has influenced the mentality of the Africans who migrate to other parts of the world towards thinking and expecting the same type of 'welcoming' as can be experienced in Africa. In Africa, because of the influence of the extended family system, people respect and have affection for one another and welcoming a visitor and treating him well is part of the culture. African sense of neighbourhood guarantees the movement of people. The issue of neighbourhood and solidarity in the African society is about a personal approach to the community of humanity where one is a person only in the company of the others.

2.3 The General Overview of the African Situation

Africa as a continent is rich in all its ramifications. The great wealth of Africa ranges from the rich tapestry of socio-cultural diversity to an enormous large reserve of the fossil fuels of the world. The enormous mineral resources are complimented by the biological resources which include a large collection of animals both wild and domestic, and large mass of land suitable for cultivation; and a good proportion of ocean and sea with their advantages. These natural advantages, coupled with the ignorance of the people due to underdevelopment and low level of education have made the exploitations of these resources the most significant economic activity in Africa in the 20th century.

The summary of the situation in Africa in the 21st century is everything but positive. The 20th century Africa seemed to show some blooming hope of improvement with the disintegration of the colonial era by the middle of the century. But towards the end of the 20th century and the beginning of the 21st century, there was a total reverse from the seemingly blossoming of hope to the stupor of hopelessness caused sometimes by Africans themselves. The economic enemies of Africa, according to Nathaniel Ndiokwere

> "are not the white people in their own countries and fatherlands. They are primarily African politicians in civil and military uniforms […] those who steal and loot their countries' treasures, and bank their loot in foreign banks from where they withdraw and squander Africa's wealth while millions languish in poverty and lack of basic necessities of life."[58]

The continent has witnessed in this 21st century, a series of social, economic, political, religious and natural disaster than in any other century in her history.

The Westerners are not helping matters either. The presentation of Africa all over the world leaves little to be deserved. The picture of violence, diseases, poverty, general decay and triumph of the evil and corruption are read regularly in the pages of the national dailies, and fill the network programmes in foreign countries. The consequences of this are very obvious. The corresponding picture of the situation in the West is not only enticing but also inviting. So in order to get out of the situation in Africa; in order to modernize, one needs to think Western or migrate. This issue of migration plunders Africa into such a stupor that the human machinery to begin a reform is almost extinct and the work ahead is as daring as it is scaring.

2.3.1 The Economy

As already stated above, Africa witnessed a blooming of hope in the 20th century, but this has its attendant problems and set backs. Agriculture was one of the factors that contributed positively to this. Some African countries exported their products and a more improved commodity trade system was also in practice then. These happened in most of the colonial territories. But in the 21st century, due to drought and

---

[58] Ndiokwere, N.I., Op.cit., p. 179.

neo-colonial influence, agricultural sector has witnessed a technical instability. Industrial evolution and more emphasis on the natural mineral resources have undermined the appreciation of the agricultural sector. Hunger is a consequence of that.

Africa as a continent is endowed naturally with the world's richest natural resources, like diamond, gold, petroleum (crude oil), coal and so on. Yet the continent is rated the poorest in the world with all the countries in it apart from those of Southern Africa. The most predominant economic system of traditional Africans is agriculture. They engage in subsistence farming. Most countries of Africa engage also in mining of their natural resources for export and partly for domestic use e.g. oil, tin, and coal.

There is no widely recognizable application of the modern mechanism of Agriculture and the state is doing little or nothing to help. This hampers the production and affects the output adversely. Poor transportation, unreliable means of communication and general poverty make it almost impossible to boost greater production and the nuclear family system in Africa makes domestic usage of farm-produce a priority.

A very serious factor militating against the economy in Africa is population. The economic growth does not correspond adequately with the population growth and this has kept the per capita gross domestic product at a very low margin.

Apart from the few Africans who enrich themselves from the public funds, thereby impoverishing the rest, some of the Western countries also contribute to the problems of the economy in Africa. These take advantage of their technological know-how and maximise their take-homes from these African countries. Nigeria produces crude oil, exports them and imports gas, petrol and kerosene. The blame for the economic failure in Africa goes to a lot of people.

The economic confusion in Africa renders, not only the continent, but also its people poor in the real sense of the meaning of the word poverty. We need to note here that poverty can be relative but there is a line of measurement in determining who is poor and who is not.

> "For technical and statistical purposes, poverty is usually measured by establishing a poverty line, ...people whose income is below the level necessary to purchase even that basic food basket are called absolutely poor...."[59]

Here we are referring to the case of extreme poverty as against relative poverty. In the Western world, inability to afford a good holiday in summer may be seen as a sign of poverty. But in Africa, the signs of poverty range from inability to pay for a simple bill for hospital treatment to uncertainty about the daily food.

The goals set by the United Nations Development Group are far fetched as far as African economies are concerned. In contrast to that of the West, African economy faces problems in every dimension. The per capita national income in Africa is one third lower than the next poorest continent which is Asia. Half of Africa's over 700 million people live on less than $1.00 a day.[60] "Africa is thus, the only region where per capita investment and saving has declined since 1970."[61]

2.3.2 Government and Politics

The Africans themselves, especially the leaders, past and present, have been and /or are still contributing to the deterioration of the situation in Africa. The political situation in Africa and the Government structures can best be described as policies that lack the aesthetics of political behaviours. A state of tyranny and dictatorship is very frequent in most of the African countries. The failure of these governments in

---

[59] Youn, K.J., Millen, J.V., Irwin, A., and Gershaman, J., (Eds), „Dying for Growth"in Samuel Kobia, *The Courage of Hope*, Geneva: WCC Publications, 2003, in 207.

[60] See *Investing in Development: A Practical Plan to Achieve the Millennium Development goals*, New York: UN Development Group, 2005, p. 15.

[61] See Ibid.

Africa is as a result of the personal and insatiable interests of the leaders to enrich themselves beyond all human imaginations from the public funds. There is a lack of distinction between what the interest of the leaders is and what the general need of the public is. This often results in a confused atmosphere which, in most cases, ushers in the military regimes through coups. Nigeria is a typical example of such. In Nigeria, between the year 1960 (when she got her independence from the British colonial master), and the beginning of the 21st century, the military ruled the country for 28years. The military has always maintained that they are forced by the circumstances to take over the leadership although they themselves are not better off in terms of salvaging the situation.

The politicians have a different agenda from that of the masses. They are not ready to debate the issue of common good on the floor of the parliament. The Politicians in Africa have the problem of understanding what the common good of the people is. Amidst the ocean of oil wealth, the Nigerian people, for example, are suffering, and have to manage, if at all, with the last drop of their blood to make ends meet. This situation is worse in the case of the minority oil-producing ethnic groups in Nigeria whose areas are the least developed areas in Nigeria. They are not only made to suffer, they pay also, sometimes with their blood, when they demand for their rights. These groups are the poorest in the country, not minding the fact that more than 90% of the wealth of Nigeria come from there. Some of the best cities in Nigeria, if not all, have no drop of oil under their ground and none has been found three hundred kilometres within their radius, as of 2007. This is also almost the same case in Ghana and her Gold, in Liberia and her Diamonds, etc. The blame goes to the governments. The problems of African nations could be seen as a consequence of the failure of leadership at all levels especially in the national governments.

It is true that most of the African countries, apart from those who are still engaged in civil war or torn apart by war, are witnessing, to some extent, the existence of democracy, the question is whether these countries are enjoying the dividends of democracy. The enjoyment of such dividends may be a goal too far to achieve. This is because the elections in Africa, where there is one, have continued to see the same people who were selfish as leaders returned unopposed due to electoral malpractices. In some cases, there appear to be a visible sign of elections but the realities are far from what they should be in terms of real or actual elections.

2.3.3 Social System

The human and material resources in Africa have not been properly harnessed, and where they have been, they are not adequately distributed. Thus, the social system in Africa needs to be re-addressed. The scandalous situations, that not only create a wide gap between the poor and the rich, but also keep widening this gap, need to be addressed.

The social security system in Africa is nothing to write home about when compared with that in Europe. In fact, there is no social security system at all in Africa. There is no health insurance policy, and the security system is still porous. The general social behaviours of the individual and thought-patterns are most of the times and in varied ways, influenced by the structures around them. This collaborates with the fact that, "the behaviour of individuals and groups is seen as falling into multiple interdependencies, and these interdependencies are 'system'."[62]

2.3.4 Educational System

Western education in general was introduced by the colonial masters. These brought education into Africa as a way of making their intention better appreciated. The people needed to communicate with the white masters and so they had to go to school. But systematic education as we have it today in most African countries was introduced by the

---

[62] Africa, 'Social System Approach', Encyclopaedia Britannica, 2005 Ultimate Reference, Op. cit.

missionaries from Europe. It is to be noted that the colonial masters built lesser schools than the missionaries. According to O. A. C. Anigbo,

> "the British colonial administration on the other hand showed very little interest in providing schools in the colonies..., the number of Government schools was too meagre to be considered significant when one evaluates the schools and colleges founded and run by the missionaries of all denominations."[63]

However, one will be forced to say that the white masters were more interested in their bid to make more business out of Africa than to give the people enlightenment. Before the advent of the western education, Africa had a system of cultural education through which the local technologies were passed on, morals were thought and the management of information and values were learnt.

Good education in an African soil is a mark of a clear economic power of the parents. The poor and average child has no other option than to go to government-owned schools which are for the public and these schools, though they have qualified teachers, are lacking basic teaching aids. The teachers do not only suffer from lack of motivation, they are also paid very poorly. Even The poor remunerations are, sometimes, not regular as most of the times the teachers will go for months without payment. Private schools offer better facilities but they are often so expensive that only few parents can afford them. Some government schools that are doing well are in practice, not for the public though in theory they are said to be. The only consolation in the educational system is the mission schools where, though the teachers are not so well paid, the measure of the training is based on the church's message of hope and good news. Admissions into these mission schools are based on merit and not on social or economic status.

---

[63] Anigbo, O.A.C., *Igbo Elite and Western Europe*, Nigeria: Africana-Fep, 1992, p. 63.

The educational curriculum in Africa places the emphasis on those study programmes for the integral development of the person on a second level of scale of preference. Until recently, the classical studies in the high schools were based only on studying European history and theories. Those who make educational policies are highly to be blamed for that.

The right to basic education should be the hallmark of the developmental plan of any society. This is, of course, not the case in most African countries as the parents have to pay for their children's basic education. It is very clear that education is not a priority in most African countries. Nigeria, as a case study places sports on a higher pedestrian than education. It is very discouraging to know that Nigeria preferred to construct a national stadium within two years, with a sum amounting to over $300 million, and sponsoring a space project with $90 million, and hosting a continental games festival, as a priority over the funding of educational programmes.[64]

The cultural and religious mentalities of most of the African countries play a role in the lack of education in Africa. This is particularly true in the case of a situation whereby the education of a female is considered as waste since their place is, in the thoughts of some, in the house. They are better seen and not heard, many would say.

It is very pertinent to note that some African governments are trying in the building up of the educational system in their countries, while others are not perturbed at all. Countries like Ghana, Malawi, Uganda, Lesotho, Tanzania, Madagascar, Zambia, Kenya, Cameroon and Benin have abolished the payment of school fees in their public schools. This advantage has helped many to go to school. Rich countries like Nigeria and South Africa have not yet done so.

---

[64] Maier, K., *This House has Fallen, Nigeria in Crisis*, Colorado: Westview Press, 2000, p.298

However, the continent still faces many problems with regard to the implementation of the policy that will enhance integral human development and encourage economic systems. The progress in these educational plans does not at all correspond with the set goals and the growing population in Africa. Education in Africa can be best described as lacking in all it takes to make a better and sound educational system. I agree with the statement that:

> "There has also been concern about the financial difficulties of the different states, the unsuitability of current educational systems to local needs, the waste and duplications in primary and secondary education, and the insufficient liaison between education policy makers and the planners of economic and social development."[65]

---

[65] Education, history of, 'Africa', Encyclopaedia Britannica, 2005 Ultimate Reference Suit (DVD).

3

MIGRATION, ASYLUM AND REFUGEE SEEKING: AS CONSEQUENCES OF THE DETERIORATED SITUATION IN AFRICA

3.1 Reasons for Migrating

In the first instance, it is widely acknowledged that migration, as an attitude of man from history, has an obvious reason why people embark on it. The risks involved notwithstanding, people are ever ready to embark on trips that are sometimes seen as suicidal. The intended gains are often seen as greater than the risks involved, or put in another way, the risks involved are seen by the migrants as being less than the danger of staying back and not embarking on the movement at all.

Migration is a response to the different situations and yearnings of human beings. It is very pertinent to note that movements in and out of Africa have existed many years ago with the Europeans being the first to spark off the process. The Roman invaders where the first to explore the continent and gave it the name Africa.

The reasons for migrating, according to Andrew M. Yuengert, a social writer, could be seen as: "A response to differences in opportunity across national borders. These differences may arise from several causes."[66] But we can say that the fundamental reason for migrating lays in the fact that man, as a moving being, can and has the right to move. But in the 21st century world, especially in the African setting, people are

[66] Yuengert, A.M., Catholic Social Teaching on Economics of Immigration, *Journal of Markets and Morality*, no.1 (Spring 2000), p. 91-92.

forced to move so as to make their situation better. Some Africans leave their countries because of violation of their human rights; others leave due to poverty, while others leave on account of unequal opportunities. All these reasons could be said to be either directly or indirectly a threat to their lives. This is just to mention but a few. In Africa, many people can no longer live with dignity.

These movements, though caused by the difficult life-situation, are embarked upon out of the free will of the individuals who intended them. But there is another form of migration which is forced and at the same time against the free will of the migrant. This is technically referred to as deportation. Deportation is the action of forcing one against his own will back to the land from where one, in search of security, had fled.

The migration of Africans today into Europe started, first of all by a forceful movement of the people against their own will into slavery. The Europeans and American merchants went to Africa and bought human machineries to boost the manpower in their industries and farm lands. It is these first foreigners who landed in the continent without Visa that first opened the way for a thought directed towards Trans Atlantic movement, and through this, the possibility of migrating gained a considerable attention. The Trans Atlantic slave trade saw some thousands of Africans moved away from their homes against their wish. "The European powers also built trading posts on the west coast of Africa, which eventually became launching points for the transport of millions of African slaves to the New World colonies."[67] However, we must also recognize other reasons which force people to move away from Africa.

---

[67] Haskins, J. & Benson, K., *Bound for America, the Forced Migration of Africans to the New World*, New York: Lothrop, Lee, & Shepard Books, 1999, p. 9.

3.1.1 As a Natural Tendency in Man

Migration will be seen only as a physical action orchestrated by the dynamism of the changing environment if we fail to see the natural aspect of this tendency in human beings. Human beings do not only move in response to the non-suitable conditions of their environment, but also in response to nature. Migration is thus a technical term given to the right of man to movement. Human beings have been known to be always on the move. A quality bestowed on them by nature. After the creation, God gave man a special injunction to conquer nature, till and multiply is a categorical imperative to be on the move.

One of the earliest views of Catholic social teaching as regards migration is that people have the natural right to migrate to sustain and to better their lives and the lives of their dependents. "Man has the right to leave his native land for various motives- and also the right to return- in order to seek better conditions of life in another country."[68] God has bestowed in his creatures this right to migrate so that the goods of the earth can reach all. Rev. Thomas Betz,[69] says, "Before God all are equal; the earth was given by God to all. When a person cannot achieve a meaningful life in his or her own land, that person has the right to move."[70] This statement of Thomas Betz, not only supports the convictions of Pope John Paul II, but gives credence to the call for an observance of the will of God who created all. "Before God we cannot excuse inhumane treatment of certain persons by claiming that their lack of legal status deprives them of rights given by the creator."[71] Expressing its principles on immigration, the Catholic Social Teaching speaks

---

[68] John Paul II, Laborem Exercens, 1981, no. 107.

[69] Thomas Betz is the director of Immigration and Refugee services in the Archdiocese of Philadelphia, USA.

[70] Betz, T., *A Guide to Understanding Catholic Social Teaching on Immigration and the Movement of Peoples*, United States Conference of Catholic Bishops, Washington, 2001, p. 3.

[71] Ibid.

out emphatically and definitively its position that every one has a right to migrate. Pope John Paul II maintained, though subtly, that a country's right that its citizens can emigrate is a mockery if it denies others the right to immigrate into its borders; "The right to emigrate is worth little if no country will guarantee the right to immigrate. Emigration and immigration are flip sides of the same coin; the right to migrate encompasses both."[72] In effect, this means that a country's support of its citizens to move freely has an implication. "[...] it is an absurdity to assert (emigration right)... without a complementary right of immigration unless there exists in fact... a number of states which allow free entry."[73]

The polarity of the human dignity and the social nature of every person extend and encompass a frame work that tends to see the countries of the world as one single human community. The world has different political systems, different economic set-ups, and different social and cultural diversities; all these, though distinguished from each other, have their role to play in bringing about a global appreciation of the different values that characterize the world, but the vision of the world as a single human community should not be neglected. In this vein, it becomes more confusing to observe that the developed world are reluctant in tolerating human movement while at the same time supporting the movement of economic order.

---

[72] Yuengert, A.M., quoted in *Journal of Markets and Morality* 3, no.1 (Spring 2000), p. 89.

[73] Dummett, A., The Transnational Migration of People Seen from Within a Natural Law Tradition, in B. Barry and R. Goodin (eds.), *Free Movement. Ethical Issues in the Transnational Migration of People and Money*, 1992, Hemel Hempstead: Harvester Wheatsheaf, quoted in Gibney, M.C., Op.cit. p. 62.

3.1.2 In Search of Greener Pastures

It is a fact that the quest for a better situation in life is the underlying factor that motivates people to migrate. This is also a right bestowed by nature- the right to sustenance.

> "For the same reason that humans have a right to privately owned goods- so that families can provide for their needs and development- humans have a right to migrate to provide materially both for the family that migrates, and for those to whom the migrants send remittances."[74]

In response to the tendency of man to use their reason to sort their problems out, migration is resorted to as an alternative to cases of poorly constituted economies. Some people's right to economic initiatives is unfortunately restricted in their home countries. These have the natural freedom and right to seek other geographical areas other than their particular areas where they can exercise and bring these initiatives into action.[75]

The dailies are all filled with stories of people leaving the shores of Africa in search of greener pastures. Poverty and bad economic situations are some of the pre-dominant factors that cause movements of people. This may be a direct cause as in the case of hunger due to varied factors, or indirect cause as in the case of one fighting for one's due right and thereby having his or her life threatened. Many people living under sub-human conditions in their homelands dream of going to a land that offers more and better opportunities for survival. "They see it in television programme and hear about it from recruitment agents. They can also be enticed by relatives and friends who are already there

---

[74] John XXIII, Mater et Magistra, 1961, no. 45 , see also Paul VI, Populorum Progressio, 1967, no. 69.

[75] John Paul II, Sollucitudo Rei Socialis, 1987, no.15.

[…]."[76] In the present day African mentality, living or having the opportunity to visit Europe is an honour, and working or doing business there is a serious economic activity. Although, as we will see in the latter part of this research work, many who have ventured outside their home country in search of this better life are of a different opinion. More Africans are migrating to Europe in this 21st Century than in any other era of the history of mankind and "high labour force participation by migrants (Africans) in Europe…is a confirmation that economic incentives remain high for migration to those market economies."[77] The people know this very well and many have left their families and homeland to earn a wage in the countries of Europe. The distances involved not withstanding. In order to achieve this, many migrate legally, for example the businessmen and women, while others do that illegally. These illegal migrants move through different routes, while others learn how to navigate through the necessary bureaucracy and swap the protocol needed for travelling papers. Being determined to better their lives economically, people "learn how to master the complex European system of visa and residency requirements, which (determine) how long – or even whether – they could stay."[78] One astonishing thing is that these migrants are more interested in the welfare of those at home, for instance, their families and relations, than in their own. The regular remittances sent home and constant phone calls are evidences of this,

> "for in spite of official harassment, forbiddingly long distances, … migrants continued to invest their own sacrifices with meaning by committing themselves to the betterment of the lives of their dependents back in the homeland."[79]

---

[76] Agostino, M., The Challenge of the Migration Phenomenon Today, in People on the Move, XXXVIII, August 2006, p. 72.

[77] Ibid. p. 68.

[78] Mcmurray, D, A., In and Out of Morocco, London: University of Minnesota Press, 2001, p. 20. Brackets mine.

[79] Ibid.

3.1.3 Quest for Protection

The massive migration of people today is based on the need for protection. It could be protection against the imminent danger to life or protection against the threat to life.

3.1.4 For Pleasure

There is a kind of feeling and this feeling is to some extent true that those Africans who find themselves outside the shores of Africa live a better life when they return. This feeling, and the supposedly affluence, that comes at the end are real motivations and propelling factors that motivate many into migration. This feeling and hope

> "sustain them while abroad and (provide) a blueprint for the good life they (hope) to lead when they (return). (They) also put them at odds with the families and residents back home that had never left and often harboured quite different visions of the good life."[80]

Somehow, the new-found wealth enjoyed by migrants when they return, or by their household and relations back home increases the tension with their non-migrant neighbours. This increases also the desire to migrate.

3.1.5 Special Reasons

Sometimes people travel because of special reasons which are unconnected with the economic life of the people, for example, humanitarian aid workers and missionaries. These do not intend to embark on the journey so as to gain, but to help others. The missionaries are obliged to obey when they are sent. Some people are mere adventurers and researchers. These also require a conducive atmosphere to embark on their businesses which in many cases are geared towards innovations and development of the world.

---

[80] Ibid., p. xv. Brackets mine.

3.2 Problems Associated with Migration, Asylum and Refugee Seeking

In the 21st Century, the international migration from Africa to Europe increased tremendously. This constitutes problems both for Africa and Europe. This constitutes also problem for the migrants themselves. They are faced with a lot of excruciating pains in their destination areas. The deteriorated situation in Africa occasioned this traffic out of the continent.

The problems the Africans encounter as refugee or asylum seekers cannot be under emphasized. Because this migration involves a radical change, it involves also a lot of suffering. Ordinarily, it is better for one to remain in one's own country of origin and seek for his or her sustenance there. This is the opinion of the Church; "Every human being has the right to freedom of movement and of residence within the confines of his own country."[81]

There ought to be a good and comfortable condition for a settled life in one's own country of origin. The viable circumstances to a sustainable development in terms of economic, education, health and other social amenities should be a priority. The frustration of these needs leaves people with no other option other than to emigrate.

3.2.1 Nostalgia for Home

At the initial stage, the yearning to leave the shores of one's country to another in search of greener pastures is high. There is, however, the indescribable desire to return to it. Because it is not easy to cut tie with one's root. Thus "migration is a journey: it involves the packing of cases, tearful goodbyes, [...] an eagerness for new worlds shot through with nostalgia for abandoned ones."[82] This desire may be in the mind or it may be an ordinary intention. But it is there. 'East or West, home is

[81] John XXIII, Pacem in Terris, 1961, no. 25.

[82] Winder, R., Op.cit., p. 8.

home' is a common adage which is well known in every culture and land. That the Africans leave theirs in search of a better living condition and even may not return there does not remove the thought of and desire for home in them.

The extended family system that is practised in Africa makes the situation almost impossible to cut the tie with home. The people who are 'out there' are constantly asked to support those at home. The former receive constant phone calls and mails from home demanding some assistance ranging from money to material things and in some extreme cases medicines.

3.2.2 Cultural and Mental Shock

As people move and relocate, they move with their culture and mentality. Thus migration, whether voluntary or not, involves a kind of uprooting of the dynamics of human behaviour which is culture. Once these cultures and mentalities people carry along with them while migrating meet with others quite different, totally or partially, there is bound to be conflicts and shocks.

Due to the nature of this movement which, of course, is a forced movement, there is little or no time to instruct and educate one in the cultural situations one will meet in the port of destination. Though for those on voluntary migration with full documents, certain information regarding the laws, customs and traditions of the country of destination are given. At any rate, shock is an inevitable experience associated with migration.

3.2.3 Problem of Language and Integration

Language can be spoken or unspoken. Under spoken language we have words and sounds, while under unspoken language we have signs and symbols. Though unspoken language may be a little bit easier and lighter due to its similarities in many countries, the spoken language is most difficult and confusing. This exposes the migrant to the danger of being misunderstood.

Without the working knowledge of the language, it would not be easy for anyone to integrate into any given society, even one's own original society. There is a problem here as many of the migrants, especially the women, due to their religious requirements find it difficult to integrate. This is so because to learn the language well, one needs to interact. This act of interaction is termed by some as an act of immoral behaviour and could lead to moral debasement.

Not being able to communicate can be one of the most difficult situations in a man's life. It is in the nature of man to communicate among his neighbours and with one another. The migrants remain in such a state of incommunicability in a foreign land because of lack of option. In most cases learning the language is almost impossible.

3.2.4 Racism and Segregations

We have to be very cautious with the treatment of this sub-section. First of all, it has to be admitted that the root cause of racism and segregation is prejudice. According to Ndiokwere, "The primary origin or basis of racism is of course prejudice. It is any preconceived opinion or feeling and is usually unfavourable."[83] The quest for survival can also contribute to this as can be seen from the situations of the foreigners themselves. They sometimes fight and discriminate among themselves. As Winder writes,

> "Many have met bitter racial hostility- though immigration is far from being a black-and –white- affair: immigrants have jostled one another every bit as aggressively as they have been jostled by the (Europeans). [...] The same unhappy paradigms are acted

[83] Ndiokwere, N.I., Op.cit., p. 181.

out today in animosity felt by some West Indians towards Africans, [...]."[84]

Even in the same country, it is not uncommon to find people being prejudiced against based on the regional divisions within the country.

The migrants are also faced with this racial discrimination. The black Africans suffer more of this due to their colour. According to Ndiokwere, "Black people's problems are being compounded not simply by the deteriorating political, social and economic situations in most African countries and among Diaspora Blacks."[85] There are a lot of misconceptions and ugly pictures of Africa in the minds of the Europeans. The picture is most of the time wrong. The fact is that an accidental birth placement that happened independent of one should not elevate someone and/or reduce someone in the presence of others. In the definition of man, race does not play any role.

It is very appalling to see the migrants being treated solely as 'the other' and not as 'one of us' by the natives. This is done mostly to the Africans not because they are from another race, but probably because they are considered as inferior race by the Whites. Sometimes, the migrants are considered as threats to the natives in all spheres of life: in the labour market, in educational institutions, in the society generally and even sometimes, in matters concerning love affairs. In the words of Dr. Castro, the undertone of the actions of the native towards the migrants which culminate in racism is 'control'. They see the migrants as "...foreigners who must be kept under control."[86] Just as the story of migration is varied in nature, so also is the story of racism and segregation. Some came hurriedly as refugees being forced to do so; others came as merchants in search of fortune. Many experience racism while

---

[84] Winder, R., Op.cit., p. 14.

[85] Ibid.

[86] Castro, see People on the Move, Op.cit., p. 181.

others don't. The appearance of a stranger immediately sends an air of suspicion across. This is so because

> "Encounters between strangers, meanwhile, are rarely straight-forward; the mingling of peoples has always been accompanied by fear, suspicion and animosity. Migration has never, not for a thousand years, been easy. People have rarely been treated as well as they hoped or deserved."[87]

Sometimes the level and propensity of this racism and segregation gets out of hand that the victims are forced to resort to violence to defend themselves.

> "[...] the Protestant refugees from Germanic Europe, and more recent immigrants from Africa, [...] in their turn, attracted sometimes furious hatred. They have had to defend themselves, sometimes with their fists (or worst). There is a shamefully long catalogue of violent reprisals against foreigners, and it is added to nearly every day. Blatant racism is deep, ugly, endemic and hard to dislodge."[88]

It is important to note that the accounts of racial segregation reported here are relative to individual experiences.

3.2.5 France and Racial Riot

In early 50s and 60s, many Africans especially those from the former French territories were brought in to France after the collapse of France's African empire to work in France and to supply the manual labour for the booming economy. These were peasant farmers and workers who were unskilled and who later on brought their wives to join them when the industrial jobs no longer flourished as before and these immigrants being there for quite a while couldn't help it. They stayed and some nationalised and became part of the French society. They

---

[87] Winder, R., Op.cit., p. xiii.

[88] Ibid., p. 4.

stayed because in general when compared with the situation at home, the immigrants usually prefer the option of not going back even though they can if they want. The immigrants in France were told that things would be normal. However, when this didn't happen, they were disappointed. There is a feeling of being seen as a stranger in a land in which one is born and despite that, one is still regarded as an immigrant, and is sometimes discriminated against. This was the background from which the situation in France can be examined and it was based on this feeling of being marginalised and the consequent actions that tended towards a confirmation of this feeling that caused the riot.

The international community blame racism for the riot in France, "Media accounts of the riots that spread across France in the fall of 2005 lay the blame squarely on a racist society that has marginalized the children and grandchildren of North African immigrants."89 But we can say that there are other factors more than just racism which are responsible for the riot. Prof. Ibrahim Badr of French studies at York University says: "The weight of family and tradition and historical background certainly separates them from main stream French society. It's not just racism. Racism in France isn't any worse than anywhere else."[90]

It is true that there is a promise of equal opportunities for all in the French territories, but the problem has nothing to do with ethnic groupings. The problem is when there is a general concentration of poverty, unemployment and a poor living condition for this group. Under this situation and condition, the atmosphere was charged and ripe for a riot. And so following an accidental electrocution of two teenagers of African decent in October 2005 while being pursued by the police the trouble began and later spread to other parts of the country.

---

[89] CBC News Online, http://www.cbc.ca/includes/printablestory.jsp. 03.10.2007.

[90] Prof. Ibrahim Badr on CBC News, Ibid.

The government approach was at first not very suitable for a defence that the riot has nothing to do with racism and segregation. The Interior Minister then, Nicholas Sarkozy, who at first ordered a suspension of eight police officers for the beating of a youth during the riot, gave an order for the deportation of any foreigner convicted of involvement in the riot.

> "During a discussion Wednesday in the National Assembly, Sarkozy said he had told local officials that they could deport 120 foreigners who had been arrested and convicted in connection with the rioting. Sarkozy previously inflamed passions by referring to suburban troublemakers as 'scum.'"[91]

3.3 Moral Decadence

Migrants who are lucky to find themselves in the country of their destination are often disappointed. Others who may manage to settle in another country, which though not their intended destinations are their last resort are often disappointed. This disappointment comes from the fact that these countries are all prospective rewarding destinations. These people sometimes end up being exploited. They are "exploited in prostitution, indentured labour, slave-like services or even extraction of organs."[92]

The issue of prostitution cannot be overlooked in the problems involving migration. In the analysis of the problem of contemporary immigration, the issue of prostitution is among the data that rates high. This is a characteristic that features steadily because of the increasing proportion of young women involved in the practice of migration away from their countries. Most of these are heading for prostitution. In most

---

[91] http://edition.cnn.com/2005/WORLD/europe/11/10/rance.riots/index.html. 03.10.2007.

[92] Agostino, M., see Ibid., p. 73.

cases, these women who migrate are engaged in a contract between them, their negotiator and the clients. They are at times employed in the areas where they could end up in undesirable activities. These people desire a serious attention to their moral lives.

Dealing on drugs and other illegal nicotine related business is often a daily affair that is being reported on the dailies all over Europe. This does not involve only Africans. It also involves non Africans as well. The root cause of these illegal drug-related activities is the quest for survival. In as much as there is no excuse whatsoever for such business, these dealers, though not all, are ready to engage in legitimate work, but are not permitted to do so. In the face of hunger and starvation they engage in drug deals.

3.3.1 Economic Problems

The figure of the world population stretches far more than that of the migrants which represents a low proportion of the entire population of the world. But due to the geometrical progression in the number of the illegal migrants, the impact of these migrants can be felt. This is so because, being illegal in the definition of the individual government according to their constitution, makes it difficult for one to work. This, as we have seen earlier, brings about some illegal and clandestine activities. Such activities are not in the good interest of the economy of a nation.

The data of the labour flow with regard to migration shows that movement of people in search of jobs are on the increase. By doing so, the labour force for the welcoming or hosting countries increases while at the same time that of the country of origin of the migrants decreases. The menial jobs which the natives of the hosting countries will not do or shy away from doing, but which otherwise are necessary for the balance of the economic activities in these countries, are taken up by the migrants, while at the same time, such jobs in the countries of their origin are left undone. It would have been the ideal if people would stay in their countries or origin and better their condition there. Since they rely on their competencies to work abroad and earn a living, these competencies can also help build up their own lands. John XXII says: "Those also who rely on their own resources and initiative should contribute as best as they can to the equitable adjustment of economic life in their own community."[93]

Ninety percent of the African migrants in Europe are under the age of forty which is the best age for productivity both manually and otherwise. The negative consequences of this mass exodus out of the African continent can be imagined just as the positive consequences to the European world are obvious.

The main reasons for the movement continue to be the inadequate economic regulations and unemployment. With the increase of the economic crisis and the ever-growing economic strategy in Europe, irregular and illegal migration grows too. Many unauthorized African workers fill the menial labour shortage in Europe. They do not find it easy too with these jobs. Most of them are underpaid, and others sometimes do not receive their extra time allowances.

In Austria for instance, the African migrants, and asylum seekers share the newspapers. A job that they are not permitted to do because they are not allowed to work at all. But at the same time, a job the citizens see as too degrading to accept. The strange thing about it is that, these Africans, and a very few number of non-Africans who share these newspapers send them even to the very doors of those who, either made the law that forbids them from working, or have the responsibility to enforce it.

> "In another, parallel, irony many of those quickest to oppose the persistent desire of migrant workers [...] are also the quickest to exploit the cheap labour they offer. Their houses are cleaned, cars washed, extensions built, coffees mixed, drinks served and chil-

---

[93] John XXIII, Mater et Magistra, no. 151.

dren cared for on the cheap, and often in the tax-evading invisible economy, by migrant workers."[94]

3.3.2 Strict Immigration Laws

Generally, the migrants are caught in the web of strict governmental laws. The complexity of this situation comes from the fact that it is sometimes difficult for the migrants to understand and interpret the laws. As a result, they fall victims to the laws. Most of the times, they are put in prison purely because of the immigration laws.

That human beings have a fundamental right to freedom is not deniable, though this freedom should not be exercised without control. The asylum and refugee seekers are those who, if no care is taken, are lost in humanity. To incarcerate them in the pretext of upholding national security is morally wrong. Imprisonment of the asylum seeker, refugee, or migrant should be as a last resort when other alternatives have been tried. It may not be too far from the truth to hold on to the view that many governments employ the prison method just to deter prospective immigrants from entering and to discourage those already there from staying.

These laws are right in themselves in so far as they are there to serve the common good. The situation in which many find themselves incarcerated because they are in a country order than theirs' happen because of the laws which state otherwise. In treating the 'Paradox of Sovereignty' Giorgio Agamben made extensive use of Schmitt's structure of the 'exception'. It cannot be argued without flaws that there is a need for exceptions in every rule because

> "...Exception is that which cannot be subsumed; it defies general codification, but it simultaneously reveals a specifically juridical formal element. [...] All law is "situational Law". [...] The exception does not only confirm the rule; the rule as such lives off

---

[94] Winder, R., Op. cit., p. 13.

> the exception alone. The exception, [...] thinks the general with intense passion."[95]

We can then say that the propagation of 'exception' is a kind of exclusion and as such it is an individual case or issue. When applied to this section on strict immigration laws, then the need for a balancing of the rule appears. The experiences of the irregular migrants as a result of these immigration laws are numerous.[96]

The Geneva Convention of 1951 prohibits countries from punishing asylum seekers and refugees for illegally entering their territories.

> "The contracting states shall not impose penalties, on account of their illegal entry or presences, on refugees who, coming directly from a territory where their life or freedom was threatened in the sense of article 1, enter or are present in their territory without authorization."[97]

This law is being flouted. Closed borders force people to cross borders without authorizations especially when they are desperate.

---

[95] Agamben, G., Homo Sacer: Sovereign Power and Bare Life, California: Stanford University Press, 1995, pp. 15-16.

[96] As a pastoral co-helper in the Astern Prison in the Diocese of Linz in Austria, I have a personal contact with the detainees. Although most of the Africans there are involved in one way or the other with drug related crimes, there are many others there whose main crime is purely immigration issue. It is appalling to have the two groups in the prison. Those convicted on drug-related offences deserve to be there, while those held on account of immigration should be released. It is a serious problem and very disheartening too for the asylum or refugee seeker that after receiving a negative response to his application and a warning to leave, if he is still found within the territory he is thrown into prison from where he is deported. Others a simply caught without legal documents and are termed illegal. This tag qualifies them to occupy a cell in the prison yard. Here, we are faced with one of the ironies of life. People fleeing their homes because of insecurity, find themselves securely locked up in detention camps.

[97] http://www.unhcr.org/cgi-bin/texis/vtx/protect/opendoc.pdf?tbi=PROTECTIONαid=3b66c2aa10. 28.6.2007.

States have rights to control their borders, but the consequences of strict control and deprivations must be weighed. Across the globe, one finds out that there are several detentions camps for illegal migrants and some exist in form of asylum camps. While we will not actually categorize asylum and refugee camps as detention centres, we will not fail to condemn their conditions which make them morally unacceptable. Overcrowded centres with unhygienic conditions worsen the already terrible situations of the migrant. In most centres and camps, men and women are kept in the same place, thus raising a moral question for those concerned to answer.

Detention of migrants on account of immigration can traumatize the migrant and bring about mental, psychological and physical damage to the person.

> "[…] periods of detention in particular leave scars on individuals who may have already suffered hardship and abuse prior to arriving in countries where they are detained. This may complicate their reintegration in society and in not a few cases lead them to take their own lives."[98]

There is however no excuse to give for treating migrants, asylum seekers and refugees in an unbecoming manner. Claiming that they do not posses the legal document to stay does not deprive them the right given to them by God as members of one community of humanity.

---

[98] Martino, R., see People on the Move, Op.cit., p. 195.

4

THE CATHOLIC SOCIAL TEACHING AND THE PROBLE OF MIGRANTS, ASYLUM SEEKERS AND REFUGEES

4.1 Remark

The Catholic Church is fully aware of her role among men as a mother. From time to time, she, through her magisterium, makes some pronouncements geared towards enkindling the fire of awareness in this direction. The church does this earnestly so that man's life can become more human according to the standard of the Gospel.

Amid the disturbances and gross injustices to humanity emanating from the ill treatment of the migrants, asylum and refugee seekers in some territories around the world today, the church has a specific message to proclaim and a help to offer to men in their effort to direct their future, and a support to give to those who think of peace and work for justice.

4.1.1 The Development of the Catholic Social Teaching

The Catholic Social Teaching did not begin to take formal shape until the end of the 19th century. This does not mean that the Catholic Church expressed no official interest in the world before then. The church did not articulate, until the time of Pope Leo XIII, her official hierarchical teaching in a consciously systematic manner. It was with the first Social Encyclical 'Rerum Novarum' of Pope Leo XIII that the theology of Social Justice and all that this implies started. The idea that man can transform and change his society positively in the areas of politics, economics and otherwise gave rise to the distinctive assemblage of thoughts, concepts and principles which became a teaching in form and social in nature. So the Social Teaching of the church, as a matter of fact, became a product of history, a response to a need, and a discipline that is bound to be.

The various historical, philosophical and theological developments of thoughts served to clarify to the church herself her role in the actions and evolution of the societies. Offering a broad theological and philosophical framework of social analysis, the Catholic Social Teaching has been developed in three inter-related stages:

- Stage 1: The first stage has to do with the response of the church to the problems of the Industrial Revolution. Pope Leo XIII's Rerum Novarum was the first action towards that. Since the period in which this Encyclical denounced in a forceful and imperative manner the scandal of the condition of the workers in the nascent industrial societies, historical evolution has led to an awareness of other dimensions and areas of injustices and scandal to humanity, and has proffered methods of applications of social justice to these areas.
- Stage 2: The second stage emerged during the Second World War and continues to the present day. It is the extension of the Social Teaching in such a way that it can confront the growing material inter-dependence of the world and seek to provide a kind of moral framework for those in authorities. This stage focuses on the areas of politics, economics and strategic issues facing humanity.
- Stage 3: The third stage is represented by Pope Paul VI's 'Octogesima Adenines' (1971). This broader stage is carried forward by Pope John Paul II. Here, the gap between the rich and the poor, the increasingly sophisticated methods of torture and oppression in different forms are all matters of interest in this third

stage. A call for action is a key point in this stage. "As far as the church is concerned, the social Message of the Gospel must not be considered a theory, but above all else a basis and a motivation for action."[99]

4.1.2 The Scope and Dynamism of the Catholic Social Teaching

The Social Teaching of the church is rooted in the life and words of Jesus Christ who came to "bring good news to the poor, liberty to the captives, new sight to the blind."[100] The Social Teaching of the church anchors more especially in the unforgettable image of the last judgement in Mathew: "I was hungry and you gave me food, I was thirsty and you gave me drink, I was a stranger and you made me welcome, lacking clothes and you clothed me, sick and you visited me, in prison and you came to see me."[101] The Social Teaching finds root also in the early patristic teachings of Clement of Alexandria, Basil the Great, and St. Ambrose. St. Ambrose said;

> "Not from your own do you bestow upon the poor man, but you make return from what is his. For what has been given as common for use of all, you appropriate to yourself alone. The earth belongs to all, not to the rich… therefore, you are paying a debt and you are not bestowing what is not due."[102]

The Social Teaching of the church draws its origin from the encounter of the evangelical message. It extends to an elaboration on the ethical requirements in the handling of the problems and situations that arise in the daily lives of men. Thus, being radically challenging and inspirational, the Catholic Social Teaching does not compromise its condemnation of oppression and exploitation at any level. In this direction, the

---

[99] John Paul II, Centisimus Annus, 1991, no. 57.

[100] Lk.4:18.

[101] Mtt.25:35.

[102] Arila, C., *Ownership: Early Christian Writings*, New York: Orbis Books, 1983, p. 66.

Social Teaching has two directions: First, it is concerned with the dignity of man as created in the image and likeness of God, and with human rights and duties which protect and enhance this dignity, and on the other hand, it is concerned with the common good of the society.

God is the basic authority behind the Social Teaching of the Church.

> "In the Catholic view, all authority is ultimately derived from God. Consequently, every state authority involves a limited sovereignty. The limitation of the state's rightful power rests in the belief that (it is) a delegation from God."[103]

Although the Catholic Social Teaching roots all authority in the transcendent, its theories nevertheless respect the autonomy of the secular. But it does not accept any view or views which disrupt the divine purpose on earth. "Against liberalism, Catholic Social Teaching holds governments responsible for the well-being of society."[104]

In its dynamism, the Catholic Social Teaching is humanistic. Not of course in the sense of excluding faith or the supernatural, but in the sense that

> "It is a collection of key themes which have evolved in response to the challenges of the day, …what informs the teachings of John Paul today differs from what informed the teaching of Leo XIII almost a century ago, even though both ground their message in the same faith, in the God revealed by and in Jesus Christ."[105]

The advantage of the Catholic Social Teaching being centrally humanistic instead of just being Catholic is that it can address issues which are in themselves not a matter of faith as well as issues which are con-

---

[103] Coleman, J. (ed.) *One Hundred Years of Catholic Social Thought*, New York: Orbis Books, 1991, p. 26. Brackets mine.

[104] Ibid., p. 37.

[105] Schultics, M., et. al., *Our Best Kept Secret; The Rich Heritage of Catholic Social Teaching*, England: CAFOD, 1988, p. 4.

cerned with morality. Its further advantage is that it appeals to all human creatures. "A particular advantage of having a Social Teaching that is humanistic is that it aims to appeal not merely to Christians but to all people of good will."[106]

The body of the Catholic Social Teaching is by no means a fixed set of tightly developed doctrines. They are systematic and contain a reference formula. There is room for constant dialogue which is characterized by the desire to teach others and also a willingness to learn from them.

The two key humanistic values which are, Participation and Solidarity, are important aspects of the nature and dynamism of the Social Teaching. The principle of 'participation' enables people to claim their rights and shape their destiny gives them a sense of belonging in the community of humanity; while the principle of 'solidarity' which is developed in a systematic way in the encyclical Sollicitudo Rei Socialis of Pope John Paul II rescues people from individualism and gives others sense of belonging. It recommends a sense of responsibility for each other. The Social Teaching is open to a variety of applications in different continents and circumstances. This is an advantage of its wider range in scope.

In its scope, the Catholic Social Teaching is also biblical. It is in direct continuity with the words of the Old Testament prophets in denouncing injustice and announcing new hope for all, above all for the poor and the oppressed, and in the words of the New Testament, it encapsulates the method of the teachings and lives of Jesus Christ and his apostle. Having a solid base in the bible, it has an ample room for ecumenical dialogue on social issues with other Christian churches, most of whom tend to rely more on the bible than on humanistic basis.

---

[106] Dorr, D., *Option for the Poor*, Dublin: Gill and Macmillan, 1992, p. 366.

4.1.3 The Principles of Catholic Social Teaching on Immigration

The Catholic Theological tradition developed three basic principles guiding and influencing its teachings on immigration. These are based on natural law, but without prejudice to the human laws as can be found in the laws of a country. The Encyclical Rerum Novarum of Pope Leo XIII developed a systematic presentation of principles of the rights and responsibilities of peoples. It commented on the situation of immigrants, and in later documents, popes and bishops' conferences synthesized and articulated the principle into three main groups.

The first of the three principles is purely a natural law base on the fundamental right of the person. People have the right to migrate to sustain their lives and the lives of their families. This right is not dependent on what and how the natives of the host country feel about the migrants who are fleeing their countries of origin in search of either a better life or security or both. It is granted that the entrance of foreigners into a country poses a threat to the nation itself because it is may not be possible for any nation to assimilate all the migrants that may want to enter into her territory and stay. To accept such mass entrance may be detrimental to the nation and to the indigenous people who may fear a fierce competition for the scarce resources, especially in the countries where these are not enough. But the guiding principle is that everyone has an equal right to receive from the earth what is required for life. The earth is given to all by God and before him all are equal. This principle is against all forms of segregation. Thus pastoral, educational, social services and other basic amenities should be provided for all and should never be conditioned on legal status.

The second principle is that a country has the right to regulate its borders and to control immigration. The church recognizes the fact that no country can accept all who may wish to enter into it and settle there, but the criteria for accepting migrants must be based on human justice.

Pope Benedict XVI says:

> "In this regard, ...I called to mind that although it is true that highly developed countries are not always able to assimilate all those who emigrate, nonetheless it should be pointed out that the criterion for determining the level that can be sustained cannot be based solely on protecting their own prosperity, while failing to take into consideration the needs of persons who are tragically forced to ask for hospitality."[107]

People should not neglect the consequences of their movement and its adverse effect in their countries of origin just to seek adventure in a new land. Every action must be done with the common good of all in view. Because of the reoccurring nature of wars and catastrophes, people are bound to move. The people's right to move demands a corresponding duty on the country to safeguard its social and economic life and to protect it from jeopardy.

The third principle is that a country must regulate its borders with justice and mercy. A country cannot simply develop its policies without an inclusion of the external relation to it. Commitment to the common good is advocated and regulation must consider people in the spirit of justice and mercy. Immigration policies of a country must take into account many other basic rights of human being, for example, the right of a family to be together, that means, the right of one party to be joined by the rest of the family. Furthermore, a policy that allows people to live, work and contribute to the society but denies them legal status does not consider justice and mercy.

---

[107] Message of the Holy Father for the 87th World Day of Migration 2001, no.3, http://www.vatican.va/holy_father /john_paul_ii/messages/migration...

4.2 Some Papal and Church's Documents on Migrants, Asylum Seekers and Refugees

In her effort to be relevant, and in a bid to be adequate in the situation of the everyday life of the society, the church has developed a body of official social teachings. Beginning with Rerum Novarum, this teaching comprises efforts by the church to read the 'signs of the times.' "The Catholic Church has, of course, always sees itself as having a teaching role on social issues."[108]

In this research work, we are going to examine briefly some papal and church's documents dealing with our subject matter especially in the context of human rights. It will be very useful to look step by step at the basic principles and overall message contained in each of the documents we are going to examine, and see how these principles are being applied to the real situation in our world today. There are of course many other church's documents which are relevant to our topic but these ones which we are going to examine, though briefly, are much more nearer to our topic of research.

4.2.1 Rerum Novarum (Leo XIII, 1891)

This document was promulgated on 15th of May 1891 as the first-known Church's document to more articulately address the social problem of the society. It will be an omission, however, to discuss the Catholic Social Teaching in any form or manner without reference to the first systematic articulation of the classical texts and references which came to be known as Catholic Social Teaching. "No element of the contemporary church's social teaching can be fully understood apart from the fuller body of teaching and belief on which it draws."[109] The most im-

---

[108] Dorr, D., *The Social Justice Agenda*, Dublin: Gill and Macmillan, 1991, p. 46.

[109] O'Brien, D.J., Shannon, T.A., (eds.), *Catholic Social Thought: The Documentary Heritage*, New York: Orbis Books, 1992, p. 5.

portant contribution of this document to the discussion of the human person is that it initiated Catholics into a discussion of the human rights in the economic order. The encyclical came as a response to the inhuman conditions of the working people in the industrial societies. A detailed study of this document will show that it is for a more humane economic and social order because it states the guiding principles which should be held by the authorities in order to respond to the needs of the poor.

When we consider the fact that the background out of which this document was issued was one characterized by oppression and inhuman treatment of workers, then it is no wonder that the document should serve as the point of departure in our research and insight into other documents on social order. In this document, Pope Leo XIII admonished Catholics to "concentrate less on politics and more on the 'social question.'"[110] When applied by reference, the document touches on the life of the migrant workers, since it is written as a response to the industrial revolution of the nineteenth century. "While this revolution was most significant for the lower classes, no one escaped its effects. The shift from the land to the city caused massive social dislocation compounded by a lack of housing and left millions unemployed."[111] We can also recall that part of the reason why people migrate is to search for greener pastures; unemployment is also another reason for migration. The encyclical denounces the concentration of the wealth of the world to a few and the debasement of the poor by the rich:

> "The evil has been increased by rapacious usury, which, although once condemned by the church, is nevertheless, under a different form but with the same guilt, still practiced by avaricious and grasping men. And to this must be added the custom of working by contract, and the concentration of so many branches

[110] Ibid., p. 13.

[111] Ibid., p. 12.

> of trade in the hands of a few individuals, so that a small number of very rich men have been able to lay upon the masses of the poor a yoke little better than slavery itself."[112]

In its strict application, this concerns all employers of labour which includes those in the host countries where migrants, asylum seekers and refugees reside.

4.2.2 Exsul Familia (Pius XII, 1952)

This Apostolic Constitution published in August 1952 by Pius XII is the 'Magna Carta' of the church on issues of migration as a whole. With its laid-down rules and guidelines on how to handle migrants pastorally, the document is a response to the need of an authoritative back up to pastoral work in this area. The document came at a time migration was seen as a danger for the faith, and many pastors, notwithstanding the dare need of the people to migrate, went as far as discouraging people from this practice.

> "Thus migration was in fact a danger for the faith, and that caused concern in many pastors who, in some cases, even reached the point of discouraging its practice. Later on, however, it became clear that the phenomenon could not be stopped."[113]

Within the framework of this situation, the church developed an organic method for the pastoral care of the migrants, and encouraged its practice. The result of this development is the Apostolic Constitution Exsul Familia Nazarethana of 1952. It is both a motivation and a boost to the vast majority of agents already involved in this complex sector.

The document, without any doubt, was conditioned by the situation of the time of its writing, that is, in the second post-war period of the 20th century. This continued to serve the need of the time until it was no longer so adequate to guide the changing circumstances of the society.

---

[112] Leo XIII, Rerum Novarum, 1891, no. 2.

[113] John Paul II, Message for the 87th World Day of Migration 2001, no. 4.

Then time came for its change when the developments and events in the international world started to set in. The process of migration of the third world to the developed world, and increase of refugee in regions affected by disaster, natural and man-made, and the quest to better the living conditions, occasioned the action of the church, and she latter responded with the calling of the Second Vatican Council.

4.2.3 Mater et Magistra (John XXIII, 1961)

This encyclical given in Rome on the fifteenth day of May, 1961, came in the third year of the pontificate of John XXIII. It was issued as a response to the social and economic imbalances between the rich and the poor. It is very pertinent to our research here because it treated the situation of the under-developed and the not fully industrialized countries. It came as a commemoration of the seventieth anniversary of Rerum Novarum.

Mater et Magistra confirms the church's insistence on the value of just remuneration.

> "Our heart is filled with profound sadness when we observe, as it were, with our own eyes a wretched spectacle indeed- great masses of worker who in not a few nations, and even in whole continents, receive too small a return from their labour. Hence, they and their families must live in conditions completely out of accord with human dignity."[114]

In most cases, this applies to the migrants and refugees who are meant to work sometimes beyond their capacity in return for peanuts. These are incapable of making reports because most of them have no legal documents to work at all. Since this type of job is technically, though unfortunately, termed 'black Job,' those who find themselves in it cannot make any report.

---

[114] John XXIII, Mater et Magistra, no. 68.

The government of the world should do more in this regard to care for the migrants in this situation since they are also considered as less privileged.[115] Although the encyclical does not make a direct reference to migration or the conditions of the refugee and asylum seekers, it touches this area indirectly by addressing the problem that causes migration, and that is poverty and imbalance in the wealth of the world, thus:

> "The most pressing question of our day concerns the relationship between economically advanced commonwealths and those that are in process of development. The former enjoy the conveniences of life; the latter experience dire poverty."[116]

It calls for assistance and collaboration between nations. The rich ones should assist the poor ones.

> "Therefore, the nations that enjoy a sufficiency and abundance of everything may not overlook the plight of other nations whose citizens experience such domestic problems that they are all but overcome by poverty and hunger, and are not able to enjoy basic human rights."[117]

In this way, "countries are urged to promote, not hinder, family unity. John XXIII puts particular emphasis on the right of the family to migrate."[118] When the man is unable to support his family materially due to the injustices in his country with regard to labour and wages, he should exercise his right of movement, "from this arises the right of the family to migrate."[119] This encyclical leads the way to a new understanding of the ecumenical cooperation of all in social issues.

---

[115] Ibid., no. 79.

[116] Ibid., no. 157.

[117] Ibid.

[118] Yuengert, A.M., Op.cit., p. 91.

[119] Mater et Magistra, no. 45.

4.2.4 Pacem in Terris (John XXIII, 1963)

This document was issued only a few months before the death of John XXIII, and it came at the appropriate time when the renewal of the church was underway with the 'window and doors' thrown wide open to let in 'fresh air' into the church. The pope relied heavily on reason and the natural law tradition in this encyclical. He sketched the rights and duties to be followed by individuals in order to obtain peace. Of the four major themes which stand out in this document, two of them are appropriate in our research work here, namely: The rights proper to each individual, and the development of the common good. The other two themes are: the relation between authority and conscience, and disarmament.

That every human being is endowed with intelligence and free will is an affirmation that cannot be denied without a serious moral error.

> "Any human society, if it is to be well-ordered and productive, must lay down as a foundation this principle, namely, that every human being is a person; that is, his nature is endowed with intelligence and free will. Indeed, precisely because he is a person he has rights and obligations flowing directly and simultaneously from his very nature. And as these rights and obligations are universal and inviolable, so they cannot in any way be surrendered."[120]

This is the first of the list of the rights due to man as a human being in his encyclical, and from here he goes on to list the others in such an explicit way that they form one group.

Denying anybody the right to exist as a human being is also a matter of violence to humanity. Thus the migrants, refugees or asylum seekers deserve the right to life and a worthy standard of living. The pope says:

> "We see that every man has the right to life, to bodily integrity, and to the means which are suitable for the proper development

[120] John XXIII, Pacem in Terris, 1963, no. 9.

of life; these are primarily food, clothing, shelter, rest, medical care, and finally the necessary social services."[121]

In the exercise of his right, man is a free being though with limitations. Man is free to emigrate and to immigrate. The pope maintains that every "human being has the right to freedom of movement and of residence with the confines of his own country; and, when there are just reasons for it, the right to emigrate to other countries and take up residence there."[122] This right accrues from the fact that man is a member of the one human family. Arguing further, the pope says: "The fact that one is citizen of a particular state does not detract in any way from his membership in the human family as a whole, nor from his citizenship in the world community."[123]

John XXIII uses the concept of the common good as a principle of integration and argues for a respect of this right by everybody. This calls to mind the idea of duty. "Once this is admitted, it also follows that in human society to one man's right there corresponds a duty in all other persons."[124] The rights and duties, which are reciprocal in nature, are very crucial to determining how the government and people of hosting nations should address, in all fairness and charity, the needs and problems of our society in which migration, asylum and refugee seeking, sometimes forced on people, are the order of the day. We cannot ignore the fact and vision that every person belongs to one single human community, and the government of the world is justified by the extent to which it responds to the needs of the whole human community.

4.2.5 Gaudium et Spes (Vatican II Council, 1965)

The church is charged to carry out the work of Christ and to offer its assistance to humanity "in fostering that brotherhood of all

---

[121] Ibid., no. 11.

[122] Ibid., no. 25.

[123] Ibid.

[124] Ibid., no. 30.

men"[125]which is its destiny. Throughout history, the church goes extra miles to share with all human beings in their joys and hopes, and in other varying circumstances that confront them. "The joys and the hopes, the griefs and the anxieties of the men of this age, especially those who are poor or in any way afflicted, these too are the joys and hopes, the griefs and anxieties of the followers of Christ."[126]

As one of the most important documents of the church, Gaudium et Spes reaches out to incorporate all the different facets of life within its consideration. Thus, the expectations and longings of the world we live in and its dramatic characteristics are identified and evaluated. One of the revelations made by Gaudium et Spes is that of a greater awareness of the duty the people have along with others in our time. A duty, not merely seen from the sociological understanding and interpretation of the realities facing us, but an in-depth understanding and acceptance of the duty based on faith. Thus the realities are those yearnings and exigencies that confront the human person daily.

The world of the 21th century is one filled with "a true cultural and social transformation."[127] These have their adverse effects in our world and the document was very particular in mentioning migration.

> "It is also noteworthy how many men are being induced to migrate on various counts, and are thereby changing their manner of life. Thus a man's ties with his fellows are constantly being multiplied…without however always promoting appropriate personal development and truly personal relationship."[128]

The promotion of the common good, which lies at the centre of the Catholic Social Teaching, is not left out in this document. It admonishes

---

[125] Gaudium et Spes, 1965, no. 3.

[126] Ibid., no.1.

[127] Ibid., no. 4.

[128] Ibid., no. 6.

every group to take into account the needs of other groups and to foster the general welfare of the entire human family.[129]

Gaudium et Spes frowns at the treatment of the 'other' as an entity different from the 'us.' The citizens of the hosting nations sometimes see the migrants and refugee-seekers as strangers who must be treated as such. But the document has it otherwise and advocates that

> "…everyone must consider his every neighbour without exception as another self, taking into account first of all his life and the means necessary to living it with dignity, so as not to imitate the rich man who had no concern for the poor man Lazarus."[130]

4.2.6 Populorum Progressio (Paul VI, 1971)

This encyclical enlarges the scope of Rerum Novarum in the treatment of the struggle between the rich and poor classes to the extent of encompassing the tension between the rich and the poor nations. Pope Paul VI argued for the economic justice as a way to peace. He also emphasizes the idea of 'one human family' of Pacem in Terris and holds that "each man is a member of society. He is part of the whole of mankind. It is not just certain individuals, but all men who are called to this fullness of development."[131]

Following in the tradition of the papal encyclicals which extol the dignity of the human person, Paul VI oriented to a transcendent humanism "with a corresponding recognition of human dignity; the recognition of supreme values and the destiny of the person."[132]

Development in solidarity is seen as one of the surest ways of minimizing the practice of emigration. When the countries of the world collaborate adequately, then the issue of one leaving one's nation is no more necessary. "We must repeat once more that the superfluous wealth

---

[129] Ibid., no. 26.

[130] Ibid., no. 27.

[131] Populorum Progressio, Paul VI, 1967, no. 17.

[132] O'Brien, D.J., Shannon, T.A., Op.cit., p. 238.

of rich countries should be placed at the service of poor nations."[133] The encyclical ended with a final appeal that to struggle against injustice is to promote the common good and a society "where each man will be loved and helped by his brother, as his neighbor."[134]

4.2.7 Octogesima Adveniens (Paul VI, 1971)

This is an open apostolic letter from Pope Paul VI to Cardinal Maurice Roy of the Pontifical Commission on Justice and Peace in commemoration of the eightieth anniversary of Rerum Novarum. Stressing on the duties of the local churches to respond to certain situations, the letter encourages all Christians to apply the Gospel principles in their lives and respond appropriately to injustices. In this letter, the pope recognizes a new social problem facing the world then. It is also to be noted that these problems are still to be found in our world today. The problem of discrimination appears as one of them. "Among the victims of situations of injustice- unfortunately no new phenomenon-must be placed those who are discriminated against, in law or in fact, on account of their race, origin, colour, culture, sex, or religion."[135]

On another level, the pope maintains in the letter that the right to emigrate carries with it the right to a just treatment irrespective of the nationality. "We are thinking also of the precarious situation of a great number of emigrant workers whose condition as foreigners makes it all the more difficult for them to make any sort of social vindication."[136] The pope, by decrying this wanton cruelty on the foreigners asserts the right of man to emigrate, and in fact the duty of all to make this right attainable when needed. He says: "It is urgently necessary for people to go beyond a narrowly nationalist attitude in their regard and to give them a character which will assure them a right to emigrate, favour their

---

[133] Populorum Progressio, Op.cit., no 49, see also no. 78.

[134] Ibid., no. 82.

[135] Octogesima Adventiens, Paul VI, 1971, no. 16.

[136] Ibid., no. 17.

integration…." Following the gospel message, he urges all to strive to maintain a universal brotherhood, and extend a hand of fellowship in love to "the people who, to find work, or to escape a disaster or a hostile climate, leave their regions and find themselves without roots among other people."[137] It is so unfortunate that those who are often forced to leave their country to find work elsewhere find the doors closed in their faces because of racism and discrimination.

4.2.8 Laborem Exercens (John Paul II,1981)

This document is in commemoration of the ninetieth anniversary of Rerum Novarum. Although the pope does not make any direct statement in defence of the migrant here, he affirms the dignity of work and places it at the core of the social issues. He however, makes it clear that human beings have the right to look for work elsewhere, even outside their native countries. This is quite different from migrating in search of security or migrating due to threats to life. In Laborem Exercens, Pope John Paul II believes that since every human being has right to work and to earn his living through work, migration in search of work is part of this right. It may be taken to mean that this encyclical treats the conditions of the human person as far as work and labour is concerned. In this regard, refusal to let those foreigners work to earn their daily living is against the spirit of this document for "man's life is built up every day from work, from work it derives its specific dignity…."[138] Laborem Exercens defends the traditional rights of labour which is "the question of finding work or, in other words, the issue of suitable employment for all those capable of it."[139] As we have seen earlier in this research work, most nations have set up strict laws which prohibit the asylum-seekers and refugees to work. These laws never take into account the qualification of

---

[137] Ibid.

[138] Laborem Exercerns, John Paul II, 1981, no. 1.

[139] Ibid., no. 18.

the migrants, and their different areas of specializations. Their only reason for enacting such laws is to protect their national integrity.

The whole issue of work and emigration was summarized in the document as a means through which a person affirms his or her membership in the society and helps in the attainment of the common good, and he should receive all necessary support to this effect and not to be exploited. Thus the document has it as follows:

> "Man has the right to leave his native land for various motives- and also to return – in order to seek better conditions of life in another country. This fact is certainly not without difficulties of various kinds. Above all, it generally constitutes a loss for the country which is left behind. It is the departure from tradition, and culture; and that person must begin life in the midst of another society united by a different culture and very often by a different language. In this case, it is the loss of a subject of work, whose efforts of mind and body could contribute to the common good of his own country, but these efforts of mind and body contribution, are instead offered to another society which in a sense has less right to them than the person's country of origin."[140]

On the areas of work, Laborem Exercens does not recognize race or colour but rather the human capacity and potentialities as a human person. There is no favour in this regard. All are one and should be treated as such;

> "the most important thing is that the person working away from his native land, whether as a permanent emigrant or as a seasonal worker, should not be placed at a disadvantage in comparison with the other workers in that society in the matter of working rights…as regard the work relationship, the same criteria should

[140] Ibid., no. 23.

> be applied to immigrant workers as to all other workers in the society concerned."[141]

4.2.9 Sollicitudo Rei Socialis (John Paul II, 1987)

In this encyclical, Pope John Paul II reviews the international relations that picture the state of global development in the social concerns of the church. The theme of 'Solidarity' was established as the centre point for the pope in this encyclical. Following this theme, the pope extols the Universal Human Rights Declaration which is the first positive move toward the achievement of a humanity based on solidarity. An awareness of the human rights and rejection of its violation is also a central point in this direction,

> "The first positive note is the full awareness among large numbers of men and women of their own dignity and of that of every human being. This awareness is expressed, for example, in the more lively concern that human rights should be respected, and in the more vigorous rejection of their violation."[142]

The international stage of the social teaching runs from the teaching of Pius XII to that of John Paul II. Sollicitudo Rei Socailis addresses the emergence of a world free of what the pope called the 'logic of blocks'.

Several ideas serve as guidelines to the pope for the structure of this document. The first of these is the preferential option for the poor. Another one is the recognition of human rights through the rule of law. He talks about an interdependence that will provide a new standard for a shift in orientation.

This social encyclical is open to an international outlook and this is in line with the spirit of the Second Vatican Council and the encyclical Populorum Progressio which this encyclical commemorates. This option for the poor which appears frequently in this document is "a tradition to

---

[141] Ibid.

[142] John Paul II, Sollucitudo Rei Socialis, 1988, no. 26.

which the whole tradition of the church bears witness."[143] This special form of the exercise of Christian charity,

> "cannot but embrace the immense multitudes of the hungry, the needy, the homeless, those without medical care and, above all those without hope of a better future, ...to ignore them would mean becoming like the "rich man" who pretended not to know the beggar Lazarus lying at his gate (cf. Luke 16:19-31)."[144]

Although migration is not the theme of Sollucitudo Rei Socialis but development; and Solidarity is used as a starting point of development, we may not be totally wrong to hold that the factors influencing migration, asylum seeking and refugee is development and lack of solidarity. If all nations were developed, it would not be advantageous to migrate, and if there were solidarity among nations, the wealthy nations would be supporting the poor ones and in this way, there would still be no need to migrate since the help one is looking for is brought to one's door steps.

4.3 The Relevance of Sollicitudo Rei Socialis and the Efforts of the Church

The presentation of the series of reflections on the human development by Pope John Paul II in his seventh encyclical letter, Sollicitudo Rei Socialis, centres on international duty of solidarity, and the responsibility of the church to the whole of human community. The entire context and background of all he is saying consist in the fact that the church's hope for a fair distribution of the wealth of the world and a universal development appear to be very far away from being realized. The document decries the various forms of oppression and exploitations in the world today. To this effect, it was devoted to reflections and comments of the situation of the 'Populorum Progressio' which was

---

[143] Ibid., no. 42.

[144] Ibid.

written twenty years before it. In making many recommendations for a better world, the pope did not exempt the developing countries themselves from a share in the blame for the present state of things.[145]

4.3.1 Solidarity as the Basis of the Relevance of Sollicitudo Rei Socialis

One can with certainty say that the core of the teaching of Sollicitudeo Rei Socialis centres on solidarity. When viewed from this perspective, the presentations and reflections on the requirements of an authentic man's acceptance by fellow man will be seen as a task for all. In her social responsibility, the church advocates for a universality of mankind and presents this recommendation as an imperative for all. She wants all to see it as an authoritative ethical issue. The issues which humanity has viewed as private affairs but which borders on social and economic aspects of the human life, have been brought to another plain and seen from another perspective as an issue for all in a global context.

The word 'solidarity' features very prominently in the Catholic philosophic principles where it is technically known as 'solidarism.' Its leading proponent was Heinrich Pesch, a German Jesuit priest and economist. The principle of solidarism rejects individualism, and finds the principle of order for the economy as a thing for all. Following this principle, though independent of Heinrich, Pope John Paul II developed the theme 'Solidarity' and brought it to another plain, a higher one. The pope represents the term as a strong determination that is persevering. He further sees it as a readiness to commit oneself to the common good because we all are, as a matter of fact, responsible for each other.[146] Each state or country has the right to its borders and to preserve its own resources for the benefit of the citizens, but the common good which also includes those outside the domains of a given geographical location should also be considered, especially those who are residing already

---

[145] Ibid., no. 16.

[146] Ibid.

within it. "Solidarism justifies private ownership and limits it by invoking the principle that the goods of the earth should serve all mankind."[147]

4.3.2 Solidarity and the Biblical Injunctions

The church has a strong hold on the Pentecost experience of the believers. Pentecost was an occasion of a real and symbolic assembling of all races, tongues and colours. At this occasion, there was no room for distinctions and the people who experienced it did not recognize any difference among them, be they Jews or Gentile, the circumcised or the uncircumcised, slave or freeman.[148] The barrier of distinction has already been broken by Christ who himself was once a refugee in Egypt.[149] The presence of a foreigner should introduce the fraternity of the brethren and bring to focus the experience of the Pentecost. It should spur on the feeling of the universality which is a characteristic aspect of the Catholic Church. The presence of the migrants is a blessing and should be seen as a fore-experience of the final meeting of all with God and in God.

Solidarity is a Christian virtue which has its root in the bible. "Solidarity is undoubtedly a Christian virtue. In what has been said so far it has been possible to identify many points of contact between solidarity and charity, which is the distinguishing mark of Christ's disciples."[150] We noted earlier that migration is as old as the human history. The duty and task of welcoming strangers is not just a Christian injunction, it is an old tradition that has its root in the biblical accounts. Both the Old and the New Testaments are filled with stories of people who were forced to flee their homeland, either because of oppression or because of immi-

[147] New Catholic Encyclopedia, 2nd ed., Washington D.C.: Thomson Gale, 2003, vol. 13, p. 301.

[148] Col. 3:11.

[149] Eph. 2:14.

[150] Sollicitudo Rei Socialis, no. 40. See also John 13:35.

nent danger to their lives. There were also occasions where the stranger just embarks on the journey for some other special reasons.

One of the earliest biblical accounts of solidarity to strangers is the episode at Mamre, a city where Abraham extended his solidarity and hospitality to the three totally unknown passers-by who stopped by his house for some rest.[151] He neither knew them nor had any idea that they were coming. He simply saw in them men who are to be welcomed, and he did that. That he persuaded them to stay and be his guest is an indication that they didn't ask to be taken. "My Lords …if I find favour with you, please do not pass your servant by… now you have come in your servant's direction."[152] For Abraham, it was a privilege to welcome the migrants. Lot, Abraham's nephew, also pleaded on behalf of his guests who were two strangers to Sodom. "Please… do nothing to these men since they are now under the protection of my roof."[153]

As can be seen in these few cases, the main point was based on solidarity with the stranger who is vulnerable to various problems and misfortunes simply because he is a stranger. The mere fact of being a human being and in need, irrespective of where one comes from, qualifies one to receive attention as a neighbour would. Not to be concerned about the plight of one in need, would seem like being the rich man who pretended not to have noticed Lazarus at his gate.[154] "One's neighbour must therefore be loved, even if an enemy, with the same love with which the Lord loves him or her; and for that person's sake one must be ready for sacrifice."[155] Thus "the exercise of solidarity within each society is valid when its members recognize one another as persons."[156]

---

[151] See Gen.18.

[152] Ibid. 3-5.

[153] Ibid., 19:8.

[154] Luke 16:19-31.

[155] Sollicitudo Rei Socialis, Ibid.

[156] Ibid., no. 39.

The book of Exodus re-echoes the story of the chosen people of God whose story began with the selling of Joseph into slavery in Egypt and the eventual migration of the whole family of Jacob into Egypt on account of famine. The experiences of the Israelites beginning with the migration of their ancestors, their lives in Egypt and their eventual escape from their slave masters which saw them as wanderers in the desert for forty years, were painful and disheartening. On account of their personal experiences, God ordered them to have special care and interest in the affairs of aliens. "You will not, molest or oppress aliens, for you yourselves were once aliens in Egypt."[157] The injunction is not just that they should avoid molesting strangers, it includes also a good handling and offer of an assistance to them: "You shall treat the alien who resides with you no differently than the natives born among you; have the same love for him as for yourself for you too were once aliens in the land of Egypt."[158] This corresponds to what we mentioned earlier on in chapter two of this research work: "But I soon saw that we all are immigrants: it simply depends how far back you go."[159] God does not tell us to do what is impossible. He is always the first to do what he later recommends; for he "loves the stranger and gives him food and clothing. Love the stranger then, for you were once strangers in Egypt."[160]

In each of these Old Testaments injunction on the love to the stranger, God constantly reminds the Israelites that they themselves were once strangers elsewhere and had experienced more concretely a situation which they didn't like and will not like to repeat. This is the teaching of the golden rule which centres on doing to others what we would like to be done to us.[161] Every man has experienced being a

---

[157] Exodus 22:20.

[158] Leviticus 19:33-34.

[159] Winder, R., Op. cit., p. x.

[160] Deutronomy 10:18-19.

[161] See Mathew 7:2.

stranger somewhere and sometime. Most people have had the experience of residing in some other land other than theirs. The injunction to love the stranger can also be a preparation for one's future condition. The endeavours of life can force man to migrate and when that is so, then solidarity will be expected of the indigenous people of the hosting society.

The spirituality of welcoming the stranger is characterized by the command of love of God. This command of love of God is presumed by the love of neighbour, for one cannot claim to love God whom one does not see when the love of the 'other' that one sees is difficult. The ground of fundamental measurement for this love of God and neighbour is the love one has for oneself. "Love [...] as yourself."[162]

The beginning of the New Testament account of the Bible opens the story of Joseph and Mary's escape with the child Jesus to the land of Egypt and there they lived as refugees. They fled and migrated to Egypt because their security, especially that of the child Jesus was not guaranteed in their land. They exercised their human right to migrate for safety. During the cause of his open ministry, Jesus reiterated in a different manner the Old Testament's command to love and show solidarity to the stranger. He promised those who saw the needy especially the stranger and migrants and attended to them entrance into the kingdom of God. "In so far as you did this to one of the least of these brothers of mine, you did it to me."[163]

---

[162] Mathew 22:39. Because of the paranoid condition of human beings sometimes, Christ changed the condition and gave a new definition of love and also a new criterion of love by his own example. Thus we should love as he had loved us. See John 13:34. Some people hate themselves and some are even tired of life and commit suicide. If the criterion to love had remained only in 'the self', that is to love as one loves oneself, then there will be no break of the injunction if one, out of one's hatred for oneself, hates the other.

[163] Mathew 25:40.

4.3.3 Solidarity and Global Undervelopment

Although migration is not the theme of Sollucitudo Rei Sociallis but development, solidarity is used as a starting point of development. We may not be wrong to assert that the factors influencing migration, asylum and refugee seeking are underdevelopment and lack of solidarity among nations. Pope John Paul II emphasized the need for a country to maintain its population and seek reasonable means to guarantee it. He stated that a country should be structured in such a way that the citizens should, on their own, see no reason to emigrate. He opined that

> "It is possible for every country to guarantee its own population in addition to freedom of expression and movement, the possibility to satisfy basic needs such as food, health-care, work, housing and education; the frustration of these needs forces many [...] to migrate."[164]

The pope's message is very clear, and that is, an intensification of inter-national collaboration to deal with the root cause of the problems that lead people to emigrate. A just global economic order is an answer to that.

Sollucitudo Rei Sociallis discusses the important steps to be taken for the cooperation in the area of development between nations, regions and peoples in order to achieve authentic human development. We cannot talk of development from a Christian point of view without considering the issue of morality. And when the moral aspect of development is neglected, then it will be so difficult to talk about protecting the rights of the people. The recovery of the human person from the dehumanising situation of being considered as an object and the sharing of development in common by every part of the world were the intentions of John Paul II which characterises his writings. He declares and maintains that the human person is not to be seen as an object. Whether he is a refugee,

---

[164]John Paul II, message 2004, no. 3 in People on the move (April 2004), no. 94, p. 20.

migrant worker, asylum seeker, man is man and should be seen and handled as such. Man should be handled as a creature with freedom and right. The connection between this freedom and solidarity must be balanced for there to be an authentic human development.

The right to migrate and the right of migrants and asylum or refugee-seekers are included in the whole process of human development. Development implies exchange, and co-relation. It implies migration, either as an idea or as in the labour force. Without solidarity, it would be difficult to import ideas and to execute foreign businesses. Solidarity could be shown as an idea. In this case, a nation is not closed up in her technological knowledge, but is open and ready to share these ideas with other less privileged nations with the view of helping them grow. In this case, information crosses the frontiers of one country into another thereby arousing curiosity, intention and demand, and influencing establishments. It is seen as labour when personnel move across national borders to do some work, either as experts or as unskilled labourers. The solidarity in this area of development is encouraging; thus works are done in the hosting area thereby helping its economy to grow and ensuring development and at the same time remittances are sent home by the migrant workers as dividends which could also be used for other developmental opportunities back home. "No one, for instance, would have predicted that the remittances migrants send home would reach around $92 billion in 2003- virtually double what is spent globally on overseas development."[165] Since the history of humanity, human beings have been in constant search for a better home, and a better living condition. They have been in search of gold, land and freedom. Underdevelopment of many nations makes this intrinsic human tendency to be exercised. Due to underdevelopment in the world, about 190 million migrants are

---

[165] Moorhead., C., Op.cit., p. 284. Sudan received in 2003 the total sum of $638 million in remittances and $225 million in aid. See Ibid.

scattered all over the world today. These are seldom welcomed and the walls and laws against them do not hinder them from moving.

4.3.4 Solidarity and Pastoral Care of the Stranger

In the spiritual dimension, care should also be taken not to undermine the importance of religion as an integral part of development of the individual person. The central theme for the 87th World Day of Migration 2001 is:'The pastoral care of migrants, a way to accomplish the mission of the church today'. It is possible to limit the term 'migrants' to only refugees and asylum-seekers, but the church while carrying out her work of solidarity and solicitude for the people involved in this situation, refers to all aspect of human mobility with the term 'migration.' In this case all who are outside their countries of origin are included.

> "The term 'migrant' is intended first of all to refer to refugees and exiles in search of freedom and security outside the confines of their own country. However, it also refers to young people who study abroad and all those who leave their own country to look for better conditions of life elsewhere."[166]

When the encyclical Sollucitudo Rei Sociallis implies that one of the greatest injustices in the contemporary world is the poor distribution of goods and services meant for all, the services here should also been seen to comprise pastoral care of the people also: "In fact there is better understanding today that the mere accumulation of goods and services, even for the benefit of the majority, is not enough for the realization of human happiness."[167] The church recognizes her duty to show solidarity to all human beings. The migrants are not excluded in this venture. Most of them move to an area or region where the language spoken is different from the one they know. These people need also to exercise their

---

[166] John Paul II, Message for the 87th World Day of Migration 2001.

[167] Sollicitudo Rei Socialis, no. 28.

religious rights and have access to worship. Thus the encyclical warns us

> "in trying to achieve true development we must never lose sight of that dimension which is in the specific nature of man, who has been created by God in his image and likeness (cf. Gen. 1:26). It is a bodily and spiritual nature, symbolized in the second creation account by the two elements: the earth, from which God forms man's body, and the breathe of life which he breathes into man's nostrils (cf. Gen. 2:7)."[168]

Understanding the church as a communion of believers and understanding the spirituality of this communion as

> "an ability to think of our brothers and sisters in faith within the profound unity of the mystical Body, and therefore as 'those who are a part of me.' This makes us able to share their joys and sufferings, to sense their desires and attend to their needs, to offer them deep and genuine friendship."[169]

This is an injunction given to the church which is further given by her to her faithful in their relation to one another, tribe and tongue notwithstanding. To this end, there is in each country, the Catholic Commission for the Pastoral Care of Migrants. This is founded on a National level within the Bishops' Conferences and has a corresponding arm in the diocesan Commissions. The aim of this Commission is to ensure that the spiritual needs of all are met, and that care is not denied anybody pastorally especially those who are far away from their homes. Thus, the church sees the pastoral care as an ecclesiastical commitment and not simply a matter of individual affairs or of a group.

It is mentioned here that the church has it as a duty to care for the pastoral needs of the people both far and near. This is a "part of the teaching and most ancient practice of the Church [...] to relieve the

---

[168] Ibid., no. 29.

[169] Novo Millennium Inneunte, no. 43.

misery of the suffering, both far and near."[170] This is a concept of faith which enabled the church to concern herself with the pastoral needs of all humanity, strangers and migrants inclusive.

The tradition of the church is engraved in the theory of 'preferential option for the poor'. This is developed first and foremost to fight poverty in the region where the people are not cared for, and then to give the poor hope. The church has continuously urged the societies from where these migrants emanate to take up the responsibilities of doing everything possible in the direction to avoid the people from embarking on a forced departure due to hardship. This they can do by making it unnecessary to emigrate. When the conditions are suitable, then migration becomes not only unnecessary, but also useless. This does not mean that the society should make it difficulty for one to travel if need be, or make strict laws against emigration. To this end, solidarity implies that the governments of the entire world could make some efforts leading to a better economic balance for all.

The stranger in a foreign land requires also some elements of morality in his life. The issue of prostitution is viewed with consternation by the church. The increased number of women, who migrate, not those joining their husbands, is alarming. There is a call to solidarity and burden sharing which could reduce this issue of prostitution. The families in the host countries could accept migrants so that all can have family. The church should also play an important role in this regard so that no one will be without a family in this world.

In a fair consideration of the pastoral needs of migrants, attention is given to the use of the language of the migrants, though it is also necessary that they learn to speak the language of the host country. As a valuable tool for communication, language is very vital to the life of the church and of the gospel. In the liturgy, and worship life of the church, language and mentality of the people are respected without doing any

---

[170] Sollicitudo Rei Socialis , no. 31.

damage to the main sense of the mystery of the celebration. "Wherever there is a group of people who share a language other than that of the region in which they find themselves- as happens especially with emigrants, it is permissible to use the language they know."[171]

The migrant or asylum or refugee seeker has a right. This right does not exclude the right to pastoral care. We have to quickly note that in as much as a contact or connection between the countries of origin and destination is not so necessary, the pastoral care of the faithful or individual believer requires such cooperation between the church in the country of origin and the church in the host country. This helps to ascertain the stage and state of the individual Christian's spiritual life as well as provide for his growth and stability.

The spirituality of communion which is the watch word for the pastoral care of all human creatures should form the framework of the actions of the pastoral agents in this direction. Sollucitudo Rei Socialis paved the way for this understanding of the ecclesiology of communion by centralising its theme on solidarity. Being influenced by the social need of the human races built upon communality, Pope John Paul II in his Apostolic Letter: Tertio Millenio Adveniente called for an examination of conscience in the form of question, thus: "In the universal church and in the particular, is the ecclesiology of communion described in Lumen Gentium being strengthened?"[172] We should recall that Lumen Gentium sees the church as one body in Christ, the church is "a people made one with the unity of the father, the son and the Holy Spirit."[173]

With this understanding of care for those who have left their homeland, the church has always toed the part of solicitude. It is logical and sensible too to help the migrants not to lose everything. That the migrant, or asylum and refugee seeker embarks on a movement in search

---

[171] Sacrosanctum Concilium, (Inter Oemenici) no. 41.

[172] Tertio Millenio Adveniente, no. 36.

[173] Lumen Gentium, no. 4.

of a better situation and, or condition of life does not mean that he or she should be neglected so much that the faith is lost while looking for daily bread.

4.3.5 Vatican Approach: A Solidarity of Concern

The church has always seen in all migrants the image of Christ and of God. The issue of migration, asylum and refugee seeking has been one of the serious topics that have occupied the church for ages. She has done a lot in this regard and is always in the forefront of the campaign to alleviate the sufferings and pains of those concerned. These victims are in a serious agony for committing no crime other than being foreigners or fleeing their homeland in search of social or economic security which is already denied them in their respective home countries. The Vatican established The Pontifical Council for the Pastoral Care of Migrants and Itinerant People as the central body for this task within the frame work of the Catholic Church. This organ has the task

> "to stimulate, promote and animate opportune pastoral initiatives in favour of those who by choice or through necessity leave their normal place of residence, as well as to carefully follow the social, economic and cultural questions that are usually at the origin of such movements."[174]

The International Catholic Migration Commission, Caritas Organisation and many other organs are in the service of these migrants, refugees and asylum-seekers.

The Fathers of the Second Vatican Council gave the pastoral care of migrants a great attention and renewed its system in a re-organized form so as to be more suitable and adequate for the nature and circumstances of the migrants which is dynamic. Due to his zeal in this topic, Pope Paul VI came up with the issuance of the Motu Proprio 'Pastoralis Magratorum Cura' in 1969. Later in the same year another document was

---

[174] Agostino, M., *People on the Move*, Op.cit., p. 82.

published by the congregation for Bishops: 'De Patorali Magratorum Cura'. The Vatican has always responded to the issue of migration in a more adequate manner. This is so because migration is a changing phenomenon that is becoming more and more complex. Thirty five years after De Pastorali Migratorum Cura, the Pontifical Council for the Pastoral care of Migrants and Itinerant People issued a document 'Erga Migrantes Caritas Christi' (2004) to define the pastoral care of migrants and strangers.

The Vatican approach to the problems of migrants, asylum and refugee-seekers is not and should not be seen from the secular point of view, but purely from the religious sense. "Obviously, this is not a sociological, nationalistic or political function, but a commitment to the church's universal mission of announcing and inauguration {the kingdom of God} among all peoples."[175] The socio-political aspect and recommendations, as far as the approach to finding a way to ameliorate the problem of migrants, asylum and refugee-seekers is an issue treated in a latter part of this research work.

Sometimes, it may be necessary to send pastoral agents to accompany migrants on their journey especially in cases of mass migration due to catastrophe of different forms. Even in voluntary migration it may also be necessary to have pastoral agents around. This type of migration can be based on either commerce or charity.

> "The importance of accompanying migrants to their destination countries was already recognized during the migration wave from Europe to the new world or to other European countries. Already at the end of the 19th Century, members of the secular clergy were sent to migrate with them. Religious congregations were also founded specifically for this purpose." [176]

---

[175] Ibid., p. 89.

[176] Ibid.

To encourage this idea of readiness to co-migrate with migrants and to foster it especially when and where necessary, the Pontifical Council for Migrants, and the Pontifical Council for Catholic Education wrote to all Bishops and Directors of seminaries to include this aspect of care for migrants in the formation of the pastors. The spiritual values and advantages of trusting migrants to the care of the pastors who will guide them spiritually in their own language and with a splendid attention based on their culture and mentality cannot be measured. It is simply great.

On a very superficial evaluation of the Vatican's approach to the problems of migrants, it would seem that the church is only concerned with the spiritual needs of the foreigners and how to sustain the faith only. But on a closer analysis of the Vatican's approach, one finds out that the church acts beyond that. She understands the human person as a cooperate entity comprising of the psyche, the emotion and the physical body. Jesus Christ's response to his apostle's advice to send the people away to buy food for themselves has always influenced the church's reaction to the oppressive actions against the strangers and foreigners. Thus, the Lord told the apostles "give them something to eat yourselves."[177] The church, representing Christ, preaches the good news to the people as Christ did, and at the same time, tries to give them something to eat as Christ also did. The church does this in the spirit of solidarity, consideration and love for humanity and especially migrants. Furthermore, the church sees in her approach to the issue of migrants the test of her catholicity. Jesus Christ came for all and died for all. His injunction is that the good news be extended to all. Geographical location, creed, tongue, colour or tribe play no role in the definition of the neighbour by Jesus Christ who defined brotherhood and neighbourhood as simply 'the other Person'.

---

[177] Mk. 6:37.

Pope Benedict XVI, addressing the Pontifical Council on Migrants and Itinerant People defined the pastoral care of migrants and itinerant peoples as “a significant threshold of new evangelization in today’s globalized world.”[178]

4.3.6 Change in Status Quo

We have already seen in the preceding sections the injunctions of the Bible with regard to the treatment of strangers and foreigners. All migrants are foreigners and strangers in the land they reside. The scripture commends categorically that they should be well treated.[179]

The church does not distinguish in this area of showing care to strangers nor does the church consider nationality, colour or creed in his vision of seeing Christ in every human. The church sees nothing but the human person in each individual. “For the migrants who are believers of other religions, the church is also concerned with their human development and with the witness of Christian charity.”[180]

Unlike the dictations of most of the legislative laws on immigration, a change in status quo to hospitality without bound is encouraged. In this way, the world will be easily transformed into a united world where all live with a common feeling of belonging to one race. The church advocates a Christian culture of welcome to the stranger which considers the humanness in the person, a humanness which overrides the bounds of distinctions and above all the stings of racism caused by living with persons who are different.

Solidarity in Christian spirituality of welcome is based on the bible and on the teachings of Jesus Christ who blesses one for welcoming a stranger. “I was a stranger and you welcomed me.”[181] If every one is a

---

[178] Benedict XVI, address at the XVII plenary session of the PCPCM &I, in People on the Move XXXVIII, 2006, p. 65.

[179] See Ex.22:20.

[180] EMCC 59, in Agostino, M., Op. cit., p. 73.

[181] Mt. 25:35.

neighbour to every one, then it follows logically that humanity forms one big family with God as the father.[182] When taken from this angle, no one should be considered a stranger within the confines of this world to the extent of denying one any form of attention.

The gap between the rich and the poor should not be there when we have the understanding that the rich is not doing an act of charity as such by giving alms to the poor but merely sharing with him what belongs to both of them. This is also the case between the immigrant and the citizen.

When dealing with migrants and foreigner, the first thing to bear in mind is that these are also human beings. We have the duty to love them, to show them solidarity without bound. We "owe them our love and respect. They are not simply people in need for whom we are graciously doing an act of kindness. No, they are members of our family with whom we are duty-bound also to share what we have...."[183] St. Paul in his epistle to the Church in Galatia asserts the undeniable equality of all humanity "[...] for you are all one in Christ Jesus."[184] We all as humans, natives, asylum and refugee seeker, or simply migrants are equal in dignity and rights.

4.3.7 Solidarity and Cosmopolitarianism of Humanity

It will not only be strange but also an unequalled mystery of a great level in this world to find out that there is still in existence any country or region that has not yet been discovered. The fact that virtually every country of the world has her tincture of co-mingling with foreigners is a proof of the fact that the world is a cosmopolitan one.

The world today is a world of movement through various means: air, land and sea. People leave a particular area as others get in there. This is

---

[182] Catechism of the Catholic Church, no. 360, see also Acts 17:29.

[183] Agostino, M., Op.cit., p.98.

[184] Gal.,3:28.

the same with the intercultural relationship. The ancient world of mono-cultural life has given way to the 21st century multicultural experiences. The experience of diversity in the cultural life of the people is a common practice now unlike before. The dressing, eating and social habit of people are being intensified now with an aspect of the culture of other regions. In this regard, the spirit of tolerance and altitude of respect for the other's identity is to be imbibed.

In sollicitudo Rei Socialis, Pope John Paul did not set to establish a solidarity that is baseless or worse still a solidarity that tends to weaken the spirit of effort on the part of the developing countries. He, in fact, intended the opposite. He maintained that "nations of the same geographical area should establish forms of cooperation which will make them less dependent on more powerful producer."[185] In fact in the last paragraph of the encyclical just before the conclusion, he stated: "An essential condition for global solidarity is autonomy and free self-determination, also within associations such as those indicated."[186]

Without the collaboration of all the international community the framework of solidarity is bound to be neglected. It is true that each country has the right to determine, protect and maintain its borders, this right, recognized by the church, should be in line with the consideration of the common good. "Solidarity demands a readiness to accept the sacrifices necessary for the good of the whole world community."[187]

Thus, a strict border control without any consideration of authenticity of the prospective migrant is an infringement of the human right to migrate. The conflict between the treatment of the individual as a human being and the right to the maintenance of the border by state should be viewed from the point of view of obligation. The stranger who just arrived in a foreign land should have what is necessary to live a dignified

---

[185] Sollicitudo Rei Socialis, no. 45.

[186] Ibid.

[187] Ibid.

and peaceful life. The state has the duty to accord the migrant a respect due to every human person. This respect is due to everyone simply by being a human being.

It is often too painful to see the agony many potential migrants go through before they could be issued a visa to travel. Most of the times, many are denied the visa. In Nigeria, for instance, people queue up in Embassies and stand there for hours before they could get access in to the Embassy to receive a refusal to their visa application or even sometimes they waste the whole day without being attended to. Thus, human productive times are wasted in search of nothing. The embassy's staff does not get it any easier as these are often insulted by angry and anxious applicants. All these ordeal notwithstanding, potential emigrants still find their way outside the country through different means. Some go through the desert by foot while others sail by ship. Those who are engaged in the business of smuggling emigrants are fairing well because of the large sum of money they receive in return. Many lose their lives through these means. This, again, brings in the issue of moral law in this regard. Here, the church gets involved. Archbishop Agostino has this to say:

> "Severe immigration laws and restrictive immigration policies, including a limit to migrant's access... have not discouraged international migration. Regarding its irregular form, they have actually helped increase it and the considerable risk it involves."[188]

This is the case because the effectiveness of modern travels and the common knowledge of the happenings in other regions is no more an information reserved for a few. Every body has access to this knowledge now. Besides, there is a claim that is unconscious in the migrant's minds that the wealth of the world should be shared by all. With this claim in mind, the people venture into migrating not withstanding the many restrictions that are given.

---

[188] Agostino, M., Op.cit., p. 73.

"The West has erected an elaborate paper barricade- made up of passports, permits, cards and forms- which aims to prevent the world's have-nots from encroaching too noisily on its haves. But the material rewards of a successful migration from a poor country to a rich one are handsome enough to encourage a spirited defiance of such rules."[189]

[189] Winder, R., Op.cit., p.xii.

5

EVALUATION AND CONCLUSION

5.1 Evaluating the General Situation

Archbishop Agostino summarized the situations which the phenomenon of migration presents to the migrants, asylum and refugee-seekers as follows:

> "Discrimination, racism ...deception regarding contracts or conditions of work, being treated as tools and not as persons, dangerous occupations, long working hours, lower pay than that of native workers for the same job, poor housing or more, non-integration into social life, and so on."[190]

It is to be noted that most of the Africans who fled home to Europe did not embark on their flight because they were bad, at least as far as we can tell. They did not flee because they were lazy to work, but because there were none available. They did not flee because there were no lives in Africa, but because theirs were in danger. It is to be understood that people move because there is a necessity for that; a necessity to live and support one's family. Where this is not guaranteed, migration is resorted to as a supreme and heroic option.

Human beings, apart from being pilgrims here on earth, have been at one time or the other as we said in the earlier chapters of this work, migrants. The difference is the degree and the status acquired. It is a fact

---

[190] Ibid., p. 80.

that many Africans migrate to Europe and this movement is in the increase in the later period of the 20th century and in this 21st century than in any other period in the history of humanity. A better understanding of the situation and a study of it will include the history of Europe itself.

The first Africans, because of the technological backwardness in the continent, did not come to Europe through navigation. They did not, like Mungo Park,[191] explore and come to Europe. They were brought to Europe through the foot-steps of the Europeans who came to the continent on exploration and for adventure. The Africans were spurred to venture in the European continent by the Europeans themselves who, with their knowledge of navigation and compass, explored the African continent thereby provoking a desire in the Africans to experiment the risk of migrating so far in search of a better life or security or even both. Besides, the first Africans to venture in the soil of Europe were brought there as slaves. As Winder (2005) writes; "The heyday of the slave trade brought many black African (in 1768 the number of black Londoners was put at 20,000 out of 600,000- a sizeable proportion, though, like all such statistics, it is probably exaggerated)."[192]

Europe was once a migrating continent. Most of the countries in Europe have performed either inter-continental or intra-continental migration. And still most of the countries in Europe are on it in this present century. It was in the last few centuries that we can say that Europe lost its status as a migration continent as such and is now a hosting continent to migrants from Africa and others.

---

[191] Mungo Park (1771-1806) was a Scottish born explorer of the Niger River. He was the government commissioned captain who led a party of 40 Europeans on an expedition to the Niger River. He died near Bussa on the Niger (now Nigeria).

[192] Winder, R., Op. cit., p. 3.

As already emphasized at the beginning of this research work, it is a common experience to notice that the very port, be it airport, seaport or just border boundary that sees people leaving it to other countries, receive at the same time people coming into the country through it. This means that every continent has a share both in being a sending continent as well as a receiving continent in this traffic of human movement classically referred to as migration.

The report of United Nations of 2002 on 'migration in 2000' stated as follows:

> "175 million people were living outside their country of birth... sixty percent of these (are) migrants. Europe hosts 56 million, Asia 50 million, and North America 41 million. On their part, Africa hosts 16 million migrants, Central and South America 6 million, and Oceania another 6 million."[193] The report goes further to break the reception of these migrants as follow: "Western Europe also received 392.200 asylum seekers in 2000, of which 23.4% were in the UK. Germany took another 18.9%. Other countries mainly chosen by asylum seekers in the year 2000 were France, Belgium, and the Netherlands. In contrast, Denmark, Sweden and Switzerland experienced declines in application for asylum."[194]

The means of transportation play an important role in migration today. The mass media often feed the prospective migrants with wrong or inaccurate information about the world. Dr. Gabriela Pizarro, UN special reporter for the human rights of migrants said: "...communication media distribute news always accurate on the economic opportunities

[193] On Population Division, International Migration Report 2002, New York, 2002, pp. 2-3, including Table 1. See also, 'The Catholic Church Among Migrants and Refugees', a presentation at the Synod of the Anglican Dioceses of Europe, by Dr. Nilda M. Castro, in 'People in the move', Op.cit., p. 176. Brackets mine.

[194] Ibid., p. 177.

and lifestyles in other parts of the world."[195] Although this statement by Dr. Gabriela has something to do with the information of the situations and conditions of life in Europe, to say that the mass media 'distribute information that is always accurate may be a little bit an over emphasis on the issue. When the Africans who are in difficulties in their home countries read these messages, there is every tendency to dream about this 'world out there' and this increases the desire to be there too.

It will be of great advantage to understand the present-day situation with regard to migration, asylum and refugee seeking in the 21st century. As we have earlier on mentioned in this research work, that many host countries in Europe, for example, Austria, France, Spain, Germany, Switzerland, Italy, and the United Kingdom are issuing severe and restrictive laws and policies in disfavour of asylum seekers and refugees, including a limitation to their access to social service, have not in any way reduced the number of this group at all; rather, the number continues to be in the increase in some of the European countries. The resultant effect instead is an increase in the number of illegal immigrants of different status. When there is a compelling need to emigrate, and the legal means of doing so are denied, the desperate nature of the situation propels one to disobey the law, and damn the consequences.

These illegal migrants sometimes pay a heavy price for the adventure ranging from loss of money, personal possession, and contact with their family, to loss of their own lives. Some who succeed in entering the intended destination may be disappointed with the situation and face the difficult options of either staying and roughing it out or going back voluntarily, if not deported, to face a situation worse than that before the migration. Some migrants are sometimes exploited or abused by the same people who, on account of their being illegal, deny them their rights.

---

[195] Cf. Castro, N.M., Ibid., p. 179.

5.2 Overcoming the Commonly Held but Wrongly Conceived Ideas

Under this section, suffice it to mention that part of the commonly held but wrongly conceived idea is the view that Europe is a paradise on earth. This is wrong, just as it is wrong to hold that all migrants, asylum and refugee-seekers are vagabonds and liars. Many have expressed their disappointments at the situation they found themselves in while in Europe. "What appeared to be a safe haven turned out to be a continuation of the old situation, if not worse than it."[196]

During the cause of this research, it was discovered that only a very few number of asylum-seekers and refugees fair better than they were in their countries of origin.[197] After he moved from Africa to Austria, a middle aged man, Bakko from Nigeria said: "Before I left Nigeria for Austria, I heard that money can be seen on the streets and some even pluck them from the trees where they grow. I am still looking for those trees after eleven years here."[198]

Undoubtedly, there are among the migrants, asylum and refugee seekers those who are bad, such as vagabonds, drug-dealers and thieves, but these are only in the minority. The majority of them are going about their humble works to make ends meet. Modern means of information, for example, Television, Newspapers, radio and recently internet sites propagate sometimes news capable of brewing the spirit of racism and hatred against the migrants. They very often

> "...give a distorted view of the effects of migration, holding migrants responsible for the collapse of health care, education or social security system in the host country. This can lead to violence against migrants which may not always be physical, but

---

[196] Njom, T., 56 years old man from Ghana living in Linz, Upper Austria.

[197] A sample questionnaire were distributed to 50 migrants in Linz, Upper Austria, and out of the 48 that returned their sheets, 30 answered in the affirmative that they faired better while at their home countries.

[198] Bakko Nassara, 44 years, from Nigeria.

more often psychological and moral, as in cases of marginalization and exclusion."[199]

5.3 A Goal for the Future

Migrants who are termed illegal or irregular are vulnerable, in all facets of their lives to many injustices and harsh treatments in their host countries. The harsh state policies on immigration should recognize that these migrants still have in them their dignity and rights as human beings. These are not given to them, but are bestowed on them by nature. These rights and dignities are independent of the human law. They are based on divine natural law. They cannot be guaranteed by the human laws but can be protected by it. This is true because one cannot guarantee what one does not owe or have right to. Because of exploitations- an attitude through which economic gains and profits are enjoyed and acquired at the expense of the one who works, "protecting the rights of irregular migrants, therefore, would be an important step forward in stopping migrants' abuse and exploitation."[200] The church and indeed all who have the capacity to do so should contribute in the ratification of the international convention for the protection of the rights of all migrants. This could be done through a development of educational programme and pastoral workshops to animate the people in this direction.

The Vatican declarations have always rejected the imbalances that exist in our world today. The Vatican has a structure for this purpose. The church has always progressed in the effort to reduce the sufferings of the strangers and in the move to abolish the root causes of the problem that propels one to migrate at all.

---

[199] Castro, N.M., Op.cit. p. 181.

[200] Agostino, M., Op.cit., p. 73.

We have, during the cause of this research work, tried to pin-point the various aspects of the problems of the migrants, asylum and refugee seekers. We identified the very root-cause of the problem as:

- The underdevelopment and imbalances which exists in the world today.
- The desire to move in search of a better life elsewhere.
- The unsuitable legislations of different countries which limit the opportunities of migrants to have a claim to the community of humanity.

All these conditions are what the church tries to discourage and campaign against. The natives who are infected with the decease of racism and segregation are constantly reprimanded by the church to think on the universality of the human race. Being so engaged in this fight for a better humanity, the church calls on the civil authorities and other international bodies to follow suit.

It is very pertinent at this juncture to emphasize the need to pay a special attention to the different stages of the business of welcoming the stranger. Being guided by the outlines of Archbishop Agostino in this regard, we look at the different stages which should not be neglected in the whole aspect of dealing with the migrants. The stages are as he presented them thus: Acceptance, Tolerance, and Integration.

The first positive action towards the migrants, asylum or refugee-seekers, is to accept them in a brotherly manner when they first arrive in a country. This first experience would later shape their lives in the host countries. The feeling of being rejected is such that can destroy one who is not solidly formed and trained to absorb shocks. Within this first phase of acceptance, one's immediate needs as a stranger ought to be met. The needs range from a shelter to lay down the head to access to offices where one can get adequate counselling and guidance.

Being accepted may not necessarily imply being tolerated. The migrants, asylum-seekers and refugees may be accepted but at the same time denied access to the neighbours or they may even be ostracised. Being tolerated, the strangers, as well as their children, can enjoy the religious, educational and social amenities provided, as the natives do.

The last but a much longer stage to arrive at is integration. This stage is normally achieved through a gradual but progressive method. The stranger is helped to avoid a tenacious holding onto his or her culture and a blatant rejection of those of the host country. Such position can ignite a state of confusion with the corresponding crisis that normally characterizes such confusions. A middle level is and should always be aimed at. That is why in the above section on pastoral care of the migrants, we maintained that the church should send pastors who will lead the people spiritually in the method common to them. These should help the strangers to find their place within the community of believers in their new habitats by diligently integrating them in a way they are used to, but they should also not be made to be locked up in it. It is important to say that they should learn to appreciate and subsequently adapt to the culture of the hosting country and imbibe what is necessary and positive. An invitation to a dialogue with regard to the conflicting ones will not be bad.

5.3.1 A Note for the Civil Authorities

Civil authorities exist for the public to serve the interest of the whole humanity. This is achieved through the maintenance of human rights. Sollicitudo Rei Socialis treats the theme of development and underdevelopment to a great extent. Development of the people and admonition to the government of the world to ensure a better life for all is its central theme. In trying to make an evaluation to the whole system in the world, it says: "[…] the actual situation of development in the contemporary world would be incomplete without a mention of the coexistence of positive aspects."[201]

---

[201] Sollicitudo Rei Socialis, no. 26.

The civil authority and indeed the society as a whole should, as a matter of moral responsibility, enhance the protection of the naturally imbibed human dignity, a quality bestowed on the person just as a human being by nature.

Special attention should be given to the issue of detention of the asylum-seekers, refugees and migrants. If they, the migrants, should be detained, it should be under a well spelt-out law and ought not to anchor on their status as migrants. When a law of the land is broken by anyone, the penalty due to such breakage should apply but the moral order recommends that "the consequences of deprivation of liberty must be weighed- the responses of states must be proportionate and must consider individual circumstances."[202] There should be a more human and moral approach to the detention of this group, and even every other person.

Sometimes there is no clear cut distinction between criminal and immigration detention and in the public eye these are referred to as the same and thus they suffer the same fate of stigmatization.

The governments of the world, while dealing with the vulnerable of the society, especially with the migrants, asylum-seekers and the refugees, should use detention as a last resort, after exploring other options. And it should be seen as an unavoidable alternative. The condition for its acceptance should be such that it should correspond to the treatment of the person as a human being thus: "It should be under well defined criteria and for the shortest possible time, with access to legal aid, doctors, family members and friends, and pastoral care."[203]

Segregation against the migrants, asylum-seekers and refugees to the extent of refusing them the permission to work or keeping them in de-

---

[202] See Cardinal Renato Raffaela Martino, an address at the launch of the International Coalition on the detention of refugees, asylum seekers and migrants, in People on the Move, Op.cit., p. 193.

[203] Ibid., p. 197.

tention for immigration irregularities, or even keeping them in camps without being allowed to come out has an economic implication for the society at large. The human skills and potentials which could otherwise be utilized to the advantage of the state are lost. Furthermore, the huge sum of money spent in running and maintaining these camps and prisons are not in any way recovered.

On their own part, some African nations are also involved in this harsh treatment of migrants. They pass several immigration laws that constitute severe punishments for irregular migrants. Furthermore, for the civil authorities in Africa to restrict the movement of Africans or be involved in the crackdown on migration is an infringement of the freedom of movement enshrined in the 1971 protocol of Economic Community of West African States (ECOWAS). The citizens of member states have right to settle and work in other ECOWAS states. Although we are talking about Africa and ECOWAS is only an affair of West African states, nevertheless, some of the migrants who are from these ECOWAS countries cross the border of other member states as they embark on their expedition to the outside continent.

Although the countries of North Africa through which these immigrants leave the continent illegally do not belong to ECOWAS, it should be noted that a constant mass expulsions, harsh treatments and restrictions of ECOWAS citizens in the form of helping Europe control migration will harm the geopolitical and economic interest of the nations. At any rate, continuing emigrations somehow serve an economic purpose and reduce the tension of coping with unemployment within the nation.

5.4 Appraisal of Other Efforts

The situation is not all negative for the migrants. There are many other institutions and organisations that are very much engaged in the humanitarian work in favour of the migrants. In Austria, there are reports about the works of these groups. Some of these travel to Africa to do the work there for migrants and non-migrants alike who are in dare need of help. Some of these, if not all of them, could have made their way to Europe if they had seen the opportunity. Some migrated to other nations within Africa and there they seek for the status of asylum or are living as one.

One of these groups in Austria is called 'Ärzte ohne Grenzen' (this means doctors without boundary). This group has worked for refugees and displaced people for more than 30 years throughout the world. The helps to the migrants and refugees can also be extended to them in their home countries where many are displaced due to many variable factors ranging from war to hunger. In such countries, the future of the citizens is bleak hence, sometimes; the future and lives of these people are fully dependent on external helps they receive.

5.4.1 Contributions and Efforts of Upper Austria

It is pertinent to state here that migrants, asylum seekers and refugees are not absolutely without help in Europe. There are people who are ready to help alleviate their pains and sufferings to some extent. Doctors, lawyers, and social workers are sometimes engaged in this work of helping them. These including the church, sometimes collect money and unwanted clothes to give to the migrants.

Since we cannot handle, in this research work, all the individual efforts of European countries in helping the migrants, we limit our scope to our findings in the situation in Upper Austria, which is a state (Bundesland) in Austria.

Researches and enquiries were made into the system and methods of work of the Flüchtlings- and MigrantInnenbetreuung (meaning asylum and migrants counselling) called 'Volkshilfe' in Upper Austria. The findings are as follows:

An agreement was reached at in a general meeting on 1.5.2004 between the national and state authorities with regard to the handling, maintenance and payment of bills of the asylum-seekers, refugees and migrants. The general cost of the basic services like room, board, and health insurance will be shared between the state and national authority in the ration of 60:40.

In upper Austria, such organisations like Volkshilfe, Caritas, SOS Menschenrechte and Red Cross are engaged in these works. The state of Upper Austria usually offset the costs. There are other NGOs[204] which also perform some of these jobs. At a glance we can outline the basic tenet of the services rendered to the stranger in Upper Austria as follows:

Target Group:

- Asylum-seekers
- Strangers whose sojourn was granted.
- Strangers who are awaiting their deportation.
- Strangers who are passing-by in Austria.[205]
- Recognized asylum-seekers and refugees – up till 4 months after getting their positive approval.

Services of Basic Provision:

- Accommodation.
- Food and drink.
- Health-care services.
- Education and clothing.
- Transportation (Amtswege).
- Transportation home and reintegration help.
- Burial expenses.

---

[204] Non-Governmental Organisations.

[205] Die vorübergehende Fremde, die in Österreich aufhältig sein müssen (Weil sie in ein anderes EU-Land transferiert werden sollen- Dublin Abkommen; Fremde, deren Abschiebung derzeit faktisch nicht möglich ist). See Volkshilfe; Flüchtlings- und MigrantInnenbetreuung.

Types of Accommodations:

- Areas of concession (hotels and Guest houses)
- Accommodations provided by NGOs
- Individual rented houses

Objectives:

- To provide a worthy and appropriate accommodation and services for the strangers in Austria who are in dare need of them.
- To ensure that these services are guaranteed during the whole process of asylum seeking, and to bring the whole process to its end.

The asylum seekers and refugees receive some stipends every month to assist them in some other little daily expenses that are not covered by the stipulated services that the state provides. Every body does not get the same amount. The stipends are given as follows:

- Asylum seekers who are living in organized camps but carter for themselves receive every month thus: 150€ for the adult and 110€ for the children under 18 years old.
- Asylum seekers who are living in an organized camps with full provisions get every month some pocket money thus: 40€
- Asylum seekers who rent houses for themselves personally receive every month thus: for house provisions, 180€ for adult and 80€ for children under 18 years; they also get for their rent 110€ for individual and 220€ for family.

The Volkshilfe sees it as an important aspect of their duty to ensure a quick and swift procedure for all asylum seeking strangers. They ensure also that the individual situation is clearly examined to ensure who gets the asylum status and who must leave Austria.[206]

---

[206] See Volkshilfe: Flüchlings-und MigrantInnenbetreuung, (Upper Austria), 2007.

5.5 Critical Evaluation

Having come this far, we need to ascertain whether migrating as we see it today worth the troubles and confusions associated with it. We also need to look into the different laws aimed at discouraging migration which are enacted by different countries and try to determine their justifications and moralities. It is contradictory for many countries to promulgate laws banning the prospective migrants from entering its borders as refugee when they have, directly or indirectly, contributed to the conditions from which refugees are prompted to flee. Gibney sees the predicament of the refugee as "the product of tyrannical governments across the globe whose violations of their citizens' rights force people to flee."[207] He did not, however, ignore the fact that some western states contribute directly or indirectly to these conditions which cause refugee movements. Some times, these actions of other countries are seen as negligible because their consequences sometimes are not intended or are hard to foresee. But most of the times, they are actions of a conscious effort aimed at some kind of gain.

> "External parties by action or inaction can significantly influence the processes that generate refugees. Refugees do not simply appear because they are persecuted by government X or victimised by brutalising rulers in weak states; such governments exist within a necessary structure of international support."[208]

Some countries go as far as using all sorts of methods to induce fear on the prospective emigrants.

---

[207] Gibney, M.J., Op.cit., p. 51.

[208] Zolberg, A.R., et al. Escape from violence: Conflict and the Refugee Crisis in the Developing World, Oxford: Oxford University Press, 1989, p. 264.

In considering these points, two functions come to the mind immediately:

- the function of enlightening the mind so as to discover the truth and find the right path to follow amid the different teachings and dictations of the different laws;
- And the function of taking part in the action to foster the exigencies of the Gospel.

In this work, we have tried to be faithful to these double functions which are not only important for the life of the church, but also a command to her by God.

We begin this critique by recognizing the fact that each nation has the right to its borders and a duty to protect it. The Christian ethics recognizes autonomy of nations and even advocates it. Entering a country illegally can bring serious consequences from the government and can cause unimaginable hardships to the migrants. True Christians are obliged to obey the laws of the land.[209] In as much as it is better to be in one's own land and fend for oneself there, the Bible does not tell people where they are to live and work, and though its principles can help people determine whether to move or to stay. In making a moral judgement on the issue of people migrating, a balanced view of the intentions has to be made. Some people confuse *needs* with *wants* and in most cases; it is these wants (unrealistic desires) and greed that motivate people to move.

The moral implications of these movements, especially long term ones, can only be imagined than explained. A man may be able to carter for the material needs of his family if he migrates far away from home to Europe, but the moral aspect of his family life and the spiritual upbringing of his children cannot be provided from such distance.

Hunger is the first sign of poverty followed by inability to have adequate medical treatment. Many people are poor through no fault of

---

[209] See Romans 13:1-7.

theirs, especially in the developing world. Some believe that people become poor because of wrong decisions. In as much as this assertion may be true, it is also to some extent a fallacy. Many people lose their jobs because of technological advancement. This can be a reason for being poor. Others have spent their life savings in medical bills. There are many other reasons too, but the most common one is corruption of the government. This is the case with Africa as we have seen in the early chapters of this research work. Sometimes the causes of poverty are beyond the control of the people.

As already stated, movement is a characteristic of man, and the instinct to preserve life is a basic one in man. Moved by this instinct, man migrates as the situation changes for worse in search of a better life. In some countries of the world, many go hungry while in some farm products are poured into ditches and farmers are forced to kill millions of farm animals. They do this because they produced more than they needed and the excess were costing those more to manage than to keep. Besides, reports of famine, poverty and war in Africa are so common. Many people are driven to starvation because of war, or irregular governmental manipulations. When we see everywhere, signs of a system that is incapable of taking care of its subjects, and also the world that neglects millions of impoverished human beings, the tendency to find some moral basis to justify some actions geared towards preservation of life becomes imminent. And one of such actions is migration.

The solidarity preached by the encyclical Sollicitudo Rei Socialis finds its place in this circumstance. It is true that no economic system has adequately satisfied the material needs of its subjects, a certain manageable level could be attained by all with the collaboration of the governmental agencies. Many have no means of getting out of the situation by themselves. Others have learnt to handle the situation successfully through different means of which migration is one of those means. The developed world should extend their hands of support to the underdeveloped ones. This is not a task that is difficult to undertake because the wealth of the world has reached an appreciable level which is remarkable but more than ¾ of human beings are neglected in the sharing of it.

There are reasons that are sufficient enough to discourage migration just as there are those strong enough to encourage it. Migration has both religious and psychological effects. This is so because

> "mobility always implies an uprooting from the original environment, often translated into an experience of marked solitude accompanied by the risk of fading into anonymity [...]. Human mobility means numerous possibilities to be open, to meet, to assemble; however it is not possible to ignore the fact that it also brings about manifestations of individual and collective rejection, a fruit of closed mentalities that are encountered in societies beset by imbalance and fear."[210]

On the religious realm, the faith of the migrant is in danger; on the social realm, his psychological stability suffers, yet we have to move from a narrow consideration of these facts to a more aptly consideration of the right of the emigrants.

This danger to the faith has two aspects. Some migrate with their faith and not being able to express it due to language barriers, they lose it. The second danger involved in migration with regard to faith is that sometimes the migrants come with their faith and try to infiltrate the host community with it. Pope John Paul II remarked: "Today the picture of migration is radically changing: on one hand, the flow of Catholic migrants is decreasing; on the other hand, there is an increasing flow of non-Christian migrants, who settle in countries where the population is Catholic by majority."[211] This is the situation in Austria.

As we said before, every nation has the right to its borders. But this right is to be concretely employed in the concept of the universal com-

---

[210] John Paul II, Message for the 87th World Day of Migration 2001, no. 2.

[211] Ibid., no.6.

mon good which should put the whole of humanity into consideration. The right of man to emigrate should also be considered in this context. The church recognizes this right and that is why she speaks out when this right is trampled upon.

> "Thus, she (the church) does not grow tired of affirming and defending the dignity of the human person, highlighting the inalienable rights that originate from it. Specifically, these are the right to have one's own country, to live freely in one's own country, to live together with one's family, to have access to the goods necessary for a dignified life, to preserve and develop one's ethnic, cultural and linguistic heritage, to publicly profess one's religion, to be recognized and treated in all circumstances according to one's dignity as a human being."[212]

Thus the church recognizes the natural freedom based on human right for one to leave one's own country and enter another one in search of a better life or to preserve life. However, it should be noted that the developed countries may not be able to accommodate all who may wish to enter into it. This becomes true especially when such entrances are done indiscriminately. Certainly, unregulated immigration into a country may do harm to the receiving community, especially to its weak indigenous people "Before the manifold interests that are interwoven side by side with the laws of the individual countries, it is necessary to have international norms that are capable of regulating everyone's rights, so as to prevent unilateral decisions that are harmful to the weakest."[213] The Pope went on to assert that

> "[…] although it is true that highly developed countries are not always able to assimilate all those who emigrate; nonetheless, it should be pointed out that the criterion for determining the level that can be sustained cannot be based solely on protecting their

---

[212] Ibid., no. 3.

[213] Ibid.

own prosperity, while failing to take into consideration the needs of persons who are tragically forced to ask for hospitality."[214]

This is a serious issue because the natural instinct to preserve life is a universal instinct man possesses irrespective of his quality and ability. To make a decision on who should be admitted and who should not, based on what one can offer, brings to question the issue of partiality. Many countries take into consideration what one has to offer when admitted. This and many other related abilities form part of the basis for a positive consideration. This is a theory of survival of the fittest, which is abhorred by the church and natural law.

There ought to be a middle approach to the debate on migration. This approach should aim at balancing the implications of migration on all spheres of life: religious, economic, social, political and otherwise. An attempt aimed at abolishing migration totally will not only be a futile effort, but also will result to a kind of catastrophic situation to the universality of the economic aspect of our world and of the general social structures. This is so because migration in itself "is a structural component of present day society's socio-economic and political reality."[215] On the other hand, governmental or legislative laws aimed at putting a stop to the opportunities of seeking for asylum or refugee status should be viewed with consternation since they do not take many implications of such moves into considerations.

On a humanitarian level, there is a lack of solidarity which Sollicitudo Rei Socialis advocates. The developed world approach migration one-sidedly. They see it from the angle of security and are doing little to stop its root-causes which are economical and political. For many people are languishing in hunger and deceases while some have more than what they need. These usually resort to migration as a last alternative. They try to enter their destinations through various routes, under appalling

---

[214] Ibid.

[215] Castro, N. M., *People on the Move*, Op. cit., p. 176.

conditions, and sometimes, as we have said earlier, at the expense of their lives. Sometimes, these developed countries give incentives to some African nations to help them curb irregular migration. These aids provided in exchange for controlling migration do not have reasonable impact in development. Most of the people who embark on this journey are youths. It is a clear fact that the youths are the future of Africa and of any other continent in the world. When they are so destroyed in the course of migration, it will not only affect Africa, but also the rest of the world. This goes to support what Nicolas Sarkozy as the Interior and Town minister of France said, "Africa's failure today would spell disaster for Europe tomorrow."[216] In that speech, one of the main concerns of Sarkozy at first was how to help Africa stand and carter for herself in such a way that what those youths of Africa risk their lives looking for in Europe can also be found in the continent. When this is so, then it becomes useless to migrate at all. "How can we restore confidence in Africa's youth and persuade them that they don't need to emigrate in order to have a future?"[217] This is the question that makes the difference. When contrasted with his statement on November 10, 2005 during the period of the French riot, when he called the rioters, most of whom are French youths of African descent, 'scum', one can see a shift in ideas. As we have earlier on seen in Chapter three, he called for a deportation of all foreigners convicted in the riot as a punishment, but only ordered for a suspension of the two policemen who beat a youth while six others were watching.[218] There is a salient action in the minister's position which may tend to provoke a suspicion of racism and inconsideration. That a question is posed here on how to restore confidence in the youth

---

216 See Speech by Nicolas Sarkozy, at Euro-African Conference on Migration and Development, http://www.ambafrance-us.org/news/statmnts/2006/euro_african_conference_sarkozy. 06.10.2007.

217 Ibid.

218 http://edition.cnn.com/2005/WORLD/europe/11/10/france.riots/index.html. 03.10.2007.

is a shift away from the common view of most of the authorities in the developed world who tend to concentrate more on how to reduce the number of immigrants than on what to do to better the conditions that necessitate the movement. When analyzed properly, this question suggests a shift away from the two extremes which have characterized any debate on migration: the freedom for all to migrate; and what Sarkozy called zero migration, that is, total abolition of the right to migrate.

Throwing European border open for all will have long term consequences. Apart from the political asylum-seekers, other migrants could be allowed to get training and experiences in Europe and use this knowledge to develop their countries. In this case, a state-to-state dialogue advocated by Sarkozy could be a way out. He said:

> "It is high time that Europe and Africa pooled their forces to eradicate this heinous trafficking, a modern version of slavery [...]. Adoption of a partnership between countries of origin, transit and destination is an extremely novel approach, opening a new era in the management of migratory flows. The establishment of a pragmatic action plan is an essential stage on the road to concerted management of immigration [...]. I'm thinking in particular of the creation of the Euro-African migration observatory [...]. And the measures designed to encourage co-development, facilitate the access of African students to European universities and promote readmission agreements to combat illegal immigration."[219]

When properly organized, the outcome of the African migrants' labour in Europe could be leverage for the continent. Substantial sum of money is being remitted from Europe to Africa by these migrants. With good help and policies, this money could give a boast to Africa's development. It is not enough to adopt a partnership with Africa aimed at combating migration; such partnership should also aim at introducing

[219] Ibid.

methods of converting these remittances into tools and means of economic advancements. In this way the youths can be discouraged from migrating. No matter the solution one may proffer, the only way out of mass migration of Africans to Europe is development and this is by the way of solidarity proposed by Pope John Paul II in Sollicitudo Rei Socialis. Thus Sarkozy says: "Long term Africa's development is the only solution, the only response to the challenge of immigration."[220]

Enacting strict immigration laws and border control has not, in any way, reduced the number of illegal migrants. Even some legal migrants overstay their visa and turn to illegal migrants as a result. "Instead of discouraging them from trying to make it to Europe, the untenable conditions in Morocco have made them desperate and reckless in their attempts to scale the walls [...]."[221] This is the situation of some people who were caught trying to make it outside Africa through Morocco.

5.5.1 Some Concrete Reports and Critque

McClatchy Newspapers

As reported by Hannah Allam, of McClatchy Newspapers:

"Antonio, 29, left Ghana eight months ago after his mother died and his father begged him to help support his three siblings. Armstrong, 31, couldn't make ends meet as a carpenter in his native Cameroon, so he set off a year and a half ago after promising his young daughter he'd return with new toys. Omar, 25, lost track of his family after rebels raided his village in the tumultuous Central African Republic. He fled his country last year with a handful of cash and the clothes on his back. Lured by tales of opportunity, all three men set out to reach Europe through a smug-

[220] Ibid.

[221] Moroccan crackdown strands African migrants on Yahoo, http://news.yahoo.com/s/mcclatchy/20070905bcmoroccoimmigration_attn_national_f. 06.09.2007.

glers' network that runs from central Africa through Morocco. Now they're stuck in this dusty, cactus-speckled hub on the Algerian border, caught by a crackdown on illegal immigrants that's outraged human rights groups but has won praise and economic incentives for Morocco from Spanish officials [...]. Each man bears scars from several attempts to hop the forbidding walls that surround Spanish enclaves in northern Morocco, yet the beatings and barbed wire haven't deterred them from trying again. "[222]

YaleGlobal Online

"Mauritania, like other African countries, offers a desperate future. Residents age with a fatalism born of a failed education system, joblessness and constant violence. Any endeavour to escape is a testament to the human spirit, and many pin their hopes on a treacherous Atlantic journey to Europe. The risk often ends in death or disappointment as patrols from Europe capture makeshift boats, rerouting them back to a coast of misery. Thousands from other African nations converge on the Mauritania coast to make the chance. Official channels of immigration to Europe are less dangerous, but equally unreliable. With an overwhelming number of people who want to leave Africa, officials routinely deny visas. For wealthy nations, unchecked immigration raises political and economic concerns. But in Africa, immigration is undeniably a human-right issue-with people willing to risk everything for opportunity, no matter how fleeing or remote that may be."[223]

MiamiHerald.com

As reported by Shasha Bengali:

---

[222] Ibid.

[223] http://yaleglobal.yale.edu/display.article?id=7473. 03.10.2007.

"Imagine somebody who hates himself, who puts himself on a path leading to his own death, but he can do nothing about it," said Kasahoun Gorabat, a migrant from the harsh desert of eastern Ethiopia, describing a journey he's made five times in six years […]. Each time he crossed, he found work for a few months, only to be discovered and deported. On his third trip, Gorabat recalled, smugglers forced him and about 100 other passengers at gunpoint into the heaving sea more than a half-mile from the Yemeni shore, where the coast guard is notorious for firing on the boats. In the dark, he swam for his life, and when he reached the beach, he collapsed on the sand, exhausted, with a few dozen others. When they woke at dawn, they found that the tide had crawled up the beach and dragged 21 weary travellers, mostly women, back into the shallow water, where they drowned. "That was the worst thing I have seen," he said. "You always see a few dead bodies floating in the water when you're going across. When you say it's a very good journey, it means only five or six people died." Last year, according to U.N. figures, at least 328 people died making the crossing. Another 310 went missing and are presumed dead." [224]

Channel 4 – News- Immigrants crackdown ad campaign

"Spain has spent almost £1 million on a media campaign in Senegal aimed at preventing illegal immigration by highlighting the risks of dangerous sea journeys that have claimed countless lives. Last year, 31,000 Senegalese reached Spain's Canary Islands on fragile wooden boats, braving 10-days at sea […]. No one knows how many have died trying."[225]

---

[224] http://www.miamiherald.com/newsworldv-print/story/256345.html. 05.10. 2007.

[225] PA News, http://www.channel4.com/news/articles/general/water_cooler _moments/immigrants%. 05.10.2007.

Der Spiegel

The Spiegel magazine in Deutschland dedicated her 26/2006 edition to the issue of migration. As reported in the magazine, migration is a catastrophe of the century and affects us all directly or indirectly

> "Auf der einen Seite, in Nouadhibou, Hafenstadt Mauretaniens, hocken schwarze Menschen im Staub und warten auf ein Boot, das sie zu den Kanarischen Inseln bringen wird. […] Sandig sind die Straßen von Nouadhibou, 400 Holzboote liegen im Hafen, Pirogen, in die sich 60 bis 80 Leute quetschen können. Und gründlich ist das Meer, windig ist es, und die Polizisten klagen, dass sie keine Funkgeräte, keine Schnellboote und keine Hubschrauber haben, um Flüchtlinge zu fangen. 1200 Kilometer sind es von hier bis zu den Kanaren, 1200 Kilometer in diesen Pirogen, die „Cayucos" heißen, 1200 Kilometer bei Wellengang und wechselnde Strömung, es sind drei bis vier Tage auf See. 3000 Migranten sollen in den vergangenen zwölf Monaten auf dieser Route ertrunken sein. Und 11,000 erreichen seit dem 1 Januar die andere Seite. […] es gibt die ruhige Tage, an denen in 24 Stunden 700 schwarze Menschen die Kanaren erreichen; und es gibt die stürmischen Tage, an denen Hunderte ertrinken."[226]

Human Cargo – Caroline Moorehead

In Caroline Moorehead's book; Human Cargo, it was reported as follows:

> "The onlookers, peering into the darkness, could see nothing, though by now the hailstones were no longer crashing down. The night's weather was catastrophic, as Nene explains when he talks about the long night of the naufragio, the shipwreck, as the people of Realmonte describe the night of Saturday 14 September 2002, when a boat carrying 150 Liberian asylum-seekers, extra-

[226] Der Spiegel, Das Deutsche Nachrichten-Magazine, Nr. 26/26.6.06, p.66

> comunitari, went down off their popular beach. It was a freak storm, the like of which he had not experienced in all his twelve years in his beach house, and the unfortunate Liberians were disgranziati, uniquely unlucky, to have tried to come ashore that very night. [...] not only could the boat itself be seen, tipped far over on its side and half underneath the water, but, to the horror of the onlookers, people could be spotted clinging to the rock. As nene watched, first one and then another slipped beneath the waves."[227]

The main motivating factor that pushes these people to venture on this risky migration is the dream for a good job and security in their lives and the future. The condition of unrelenting war in some part and the hopeless privation of a better life in other parts of the Africans are factors to reckon with on this issue of embarking on a journey that is not just far away, but dangerous too, often across a roiling, shark-infested sea or a dry-sandy desert. The smugglers park these migrants into small boats meant only for fishing and which are not well-equipped for the high sea transport. The only aspect of technology in these boats is that they are motorized.

> "Hundreds of migrants each year don't survive the illegal crossing. Many die of dehydration during the two-night journey, their bodies thrown overboard by smugglers to lighten the load. Others are weak swimmers who drown if their boat fails or while trying to swim the last few hundred yards to shore."[228]

Those who made it across are not sure of tomorrow. This illegal journey is often characterized by constant threat of deportation. This is a kind of new slavery. The difference is that in the early slavery, the people were forced into migration, but this time they move into it them-

---

[227] Moorehead, C., *Human Cargo*, London: Vintage Books, 2006, p. 44.

[228] http://www.miamiherald.com/news/world/v-print/story/256345.html. 05.10. 2007.

selves. The risks are almost the same for the old slavery as well as for the new one. During the early slave trade, the captains of the slave ship often threw sick Africans overboard to lessen the weight of the ship as well as prevent diseases from spreading. These bodies were being eaten by sharks and other fishes.

> "During the years of the African slave trade, the seas near slave-holding installations on the African coast became especially attractive to sharks, which recognized a good feeding ground when they found one. Sharks often followed slave ships across the Atlantic, waiting for people to jump or be thrown overboard."[229]

There is a growing fear that the dangerous journey is not in any way reducing even though governments are doing a lot to stop it. For instance, in the port city of Ethiopia where many Africans are waiting to leave the continent, traditionally, the migrants are young men from Somalia and Ethiopia. But in the recent times, they come from Kenya, Uganda and Tanzania. This is a sign that the route is growing and getting more established.

Resorting to mass deportation of these migrants or refusing them work-permit is not the only solution to the situation. Experiences and reports from the past actions show that the effort will always fail. This is so because these migrants arrive without identification and sometimes for fear of going back, they refuse to give their full names or any at all, thereby refusing to let anybody know their nationalities. In an interview with *Der Spiegel*, Ayaan Hirsi Ali[230] gave a reason for that as we have just mentioned thus:

Spiegel: You gave a false identity when you applied for asylum.

---

[229] Haskins, J., & Benson, K., Op.cit., p. 28.

[230] Ayaan Hirsi Ali is a daughter of a Somalian exiled politician who migrated to the Netherlands as an asylum seeker. She was elected into the parliament in the Netherlands having contested for the post as a citizen.

Hirsi Ali: I wanted to cover my track for fear of my family. Many refugees give the wrong story. So you shouldn't even ask them about it.[231]

Although sometimes these migrants are identified by their accents and facial built, this can be confusing and in most cases can cause an international problem between nations. For instance, a country may refuse people without proper identification in the case of repatriation entrance into their territory. Furthermore, these migrants take to dangerous route because of the harsh crackdown on illegal migrants and difficulties involved in the procurement of visa for a legitimate travel.

The critical issue remains the fact that, in spite of all these efforts to stop irregular migration, the number of such illegal migrants continues to increase. For instance as reported in the Migration Information Source:

> "Rather than curbing immigration, increasing surveillance in the Strait of Gibraltar and elsewhere has led to a general diversification in attempted crossing points since 1999. Migrants now increasingly make the journey by sea from more eastern places on the Moroccan coast to mainland Spain [...]. Policies to stop migrants from coming have also had a series of unintended, counterproductive effects. [...] the use of more diverse and longer sea routes has vastly increased the area that EU countries feel they must monitor to "combat" irregular migration. [...] smuggling methods have become more professional, with smugglers using larger and faster custom-made boats and zodiacs instead of vulnerable fishing boats."[232]

And as was said before, the increasing gap between the poor and the rich plays a great role in the decision to migrate for a better living else-

---

[231] Der Spiegel, Das Deutsche Nachrichten-Magazin, Nr.26/26.6.06.

[232] http://www.migrationinformation.org/Feature/display.cfm?id=484. 06.10. 2007.

where. As Moorehead would put it; "And migration can only increase, say demographers, as high levels of insecurity and increasing disparity between rich and poor in so many parts of the world make families keen to send their children to safer and more stable economies."[233]

5.6 Conclusion

The principles of true humanism even in the face of genuinely felt solidarity can be misunderstood and wrongly applied. This is the situation with the issue of an apparent effort to make it unnecessary for the Africans to migrate. Migration is a problem of the 21st Century. It has been a problem before but not in the magnitude of this 21st Century's case. The issue of asylum-seekers, refugees and migrants has been a serious topic in the recent times. As we have noted earlier, there have always been people on the move, moving to and fro their home land for various reasons which can be summed up as; 'a quest for life'. "Ever since the sixteenth century, people have moved to work, to explore, to travel, to find better lives. What no one quite anticipated was the emergence of new multicultural societies, nor the new patterns that migration has taken."[234] We have tried in this research to advocate a position that should aim at achieving two things thus: Avoidance of a selfish particularism and oppressive liberalism; and recognition of oneness of humanity and solidarity in development.

That there are still people in the world who, in spite the difficulties involved in the irregular migration across the border of one nation to the other even at the risk of their lives, wish to embark on the journey is a sign that something is wrong in our world. The lack of solidarity as suggested by Pope John Paul II in the encyclical Sollicitudo Rei Socialis is a factor to reckon with in this direction.

---

[233] Moorehead, C., Op.cit., p. 286.

[234] Moorehead, C., Op. cit., p. 283.

The nations of the developed world will be guilty of a selfish particularism when they consider only their welfare in closing their door to the others. The common good which each law should serve extends, to some extent, to the other members of the human family. Knowing that these migrants are escaping either persecution, mostly by government, or life threatening situations, it becomes an action against morality and sacredness of life to send them back to the very system that wants them dead. Sometimes there are situations where the migrants tell lots of lies and present cases of persecutions and threats to their lives. As Moorehead puts it; "I started with no preconceived ideas, beyond recognition that among the asylum-seekers there are certainly people who have no history of persecution, and that not everything said to me would be true."[235] That is why there ought to be thorough procedures in the handling of the issues concerning migrants bearing in mind that abuse does not take away use. In this regard, the work of those conducting the interviews to determine who should receive the status of asylum and who should not receive it should not only be to look out for lies and inconsistencies in the testimonies of the asylum seekers.

Being liberal to strangers and migrants will be seen as oppression if because of their lack of status, they are exploited. Some countries may admit migrants because of the cheap labour they offer and being desperate and vulnerable are ready to do any job for any amount, and even sometimes just for food. It becomes an oppressive liberalism when these migrants are welcomed with the intention of exploiting them.

> "Most work and live in highly degrading circumstances in overcrowded houses or, sometimes, in improvised camps. They are generally denied access to legal assistance and schooling. Those

---

[235] Ibid., p. 4.

working in the informal economies of Spain and Italy are also subject to severe exploitation and abuse by their employers."[236]

There are also possibilities of government being under pressure by the employers demand for unskilled labourers which implies allowing more legal migrants to come or legalizing those already within.

The church seeks to lead the people to a full realization of their role as builders of the human society, agents of development and advocates of solidarity among one another. That the right to economic initiative is being constantly trampled upon is a known fact and this is one of the rights that would benefit all if handled well. In an unconscious following of the dictates of the encyclical Sollicitudo Rei Socialis, most countries of the world act in a positive way to allay the pains of these irregular migrants. But sometimes this is met with consternation from other countries. In Africa, Morocco

> "...officially blames Algeria for tacitly allowing sub-Saharans to migrate over its territory."[237] In Europe, Spain is blamed for "regularizing about 600,000 migrants in 2005, which they believe attracts more irregular migrants. Spain has called this response 'demagogic,' pointing out that, in the past, most EU Member States felt compelled to revert to similar regularizations of their *de facto* settled undocumented migrant labour force."[238]

Following the complexity of the issue, any harsh action aimed at stopping the human traffic will always meet with some kind of hindrance. The solution will rather be a tacit action aimed at a control rather than abolition and it must be based on a common collaboration of all nations in the development of the world. Knowing and feeling that the

---

[236] http://www.migrationinformation.org/Feature/display.cfm?id=484. 06.10. 2007.

[237] Ibid.

[238] Ibid.

world is linked together in a common destiny, nations should work together to avoid the anguish of anxiety and deprivation.

The sovereignty of a country ought to be respected by all. And the irregular migrants have a part to play in this call for respect while reacting naturally to the human instinct to preserve life. Bearing in mind that there may never be a time a full development will be met for all in an equal grade, the encyclical Sollicitudo Rei Socialis making an analysis of the Familiaris Consortio, reminds us that "development is not a straight-forward process, as it were automatic and in itself limitless, as though, given certain conditions, the human race were able to progress rapidly towards and undefined perfection of some kind."[239]

If the nations and people of the world fail to collaborate in the spirit of solidarity, none of what has been proposed or examined in this research work can be achieved. With the understanding of the term 'solidarity' as used and recommended in Sollicitudo Rei Socialis with regard to development of the world, the autonomy of man can be achieved to some extent because "solidarity demands a readiness to accept the sacrifices necessary for the good of the whole world community."[240] This is true in the real sense of it for as people yearn for a better life, nations ought to bear that in mind. It cannot be denied that it would be good if the situations that necessitate migration could be prevented from occurring. When this happens, then people will stop migrating. And those who have already migrated will return home.

> "But until the improbable day comes when they are able to return home, refugees will keep on moving, and governments have no alternative but to find policies which protect their borders, but which are also humane and protect the rights of those who seek asylum. […] Protecting people who flee persecution is a respon-

---

[239] John Paul II, Sollicitudo Rei Socialis, no.27. See also Familiaris Consortio, no. 6.

[240] Ibid.

> sibility all nation states have to share if collective sovereignty is to have some moral worth."[241]

Not to accept a migrant, amount to worsening his situation especially when he is fleeing from persecution and threat to his life. It amounts to denying him a position. The migrant in this situation finds himself living in the middle of two worlds: the world of his destination which has refused him settlement and the world of his port of departure into which he will not go. This is a situation Hannah Arendt describes as a condition which makes the migrants

> "[...] groups of people who were not only forced to flee their traditional homeland but simultaneously deprived of any reasonable prospect of attaining a new one.[242] It is necessity that drives one away from one's home for taking all things to be equal; no one would leave his home. No one, in the end wants to be a refugee. Exile is an unhappy state. Refugees seldom want to leave home. And when forced to do so, they dream of the day they can return. The best 'durable solution' for any refugee is to go home, but to a home and a country that are safe; if that is impossible, the next best option is resettlement. [...] in an age of globalisation, it is simply not possible to ignore the world's dispossessed. How a state deals with its refugees should be a measure of its social and political health."[243]

However, as the world grows more conscious of the apparent danger posed by migration, and some natural barriers get more porous, the developed nations enacts laws aimed at barricading the desperate migrants from immigrating. The church tries to balance the two sides by proposing the spirit of solidarity among all for in one way or the other, we all "have immigrant ancestors somewhere in the dense foliage of our

---

[241] Moorehead, C., Op.cit. p. 289.

[242] Arendt, H., Op.cit., pp. 293-294.

[243] Ibid.

family trees, whether we like it or not. [...]. Many of our most popular trees and flowers are immigrants."[244] With this fact in mind, an attempt should be made to balance the recalcitrance of the irregular migrants and the absurdity of most of the laws against migration.

---

[244] Winder R., Op.cit., p. 10.

BIBLIOGRAPHY

Agamben, G. 1995. *Homo Sacer: Sovereign Power and Bare Life*, California Standford University Press.

Anigbo, O. A.C. 1991. *Igbo Elite and Western Europe*, Onitsha Nigeria: African Fep Publishers.

Anyanwu, S.E.N. 1976. *The Igbo Family Life and Cultural Change*, Unpublished Thesis, University of Marburg.

Arendt, H. 1979. *The Origin of Totalitarianism*, New York: Harcourt Brace Jovonovich.

Arila, C. 1983. *Ownership: Early Christian Writings*, New York: Orbis Books

Barry B. and Goodin, R. (eds). 1992. *Free Movement. Ethical Issues in the Transnational Migration of People and Money*, Hemel Hepsteal: Harvester Wheatsheaf.

Coleman, J. (ed.). 1991. *One Hundred Years of Catholic Social Thought*, New York: Orbis Books.

Debirri, E., Hug J., Henriot, P., Schultheis, M. 1992. *Catholic Social Teaching, Our Best Kept Secret*, New York: Orbis Books.

Diamond, J., 1999. *Guns, Germs and Steel. The Fates of Human Societies*, New York: W.W. Norton and Company.

Dorr, D. 1991. *The Social Justice Agenda*, Dublin: Gill and Macmillan.

Dorr, D. 1992. *Option for the Poor*, Dublin: Gill and Macmillan.

Ejiofor, L. U. 1982. *Igbo Kingdoms, Power and Control*, Onitsha Nigeria: Africanan Fep Publishers.

Gibney, M. (ed.). 1988. *Open Borders? Clossed Societies?: The Ethical and Political Issues*, Westport: Greenwood Press.

Gibney, M. J. 2004. *The Ethicas and Politics of Asylum*, New York: Cambridge University Press.

Haskin, J., and Benson, K. 1999. *Bound for America, the Forced Migration of Africans in the New World*, New York: Lthrop, Lee, and Shepherd Books.

Ike, O. F., (ed.). 2004. *Globalization and African Self-Determination; what is our Future?*, Enugu: CIDJAP Publications.

Ilo, S. Chu. 2006. *The Face of Africa, Looking beyond the Shadows*, USA: AuthorHouse UK.

Jell-Bahlsen, S. 1980. *Social Integration in the Absence of the State: a Case Study of the Igbo Speaking Peoples of South Eastern Nigeria*, unpublished thesis, Berlin.

Jordan, J. 1949. *Bishop Shanahan of Southern Nigeria*, Dublin.

Kobia, S. 2003. *The Courage of Hope*, Geneva: WCC Publications.

Maier, K. 2000. *This House has Fallen, Nigeria in Crisis*, Coloredo: Westview Press.

Mazuri, A. 1977. *Africa's International Relations*, London: Heinemann Educational Books.

Mbefo, L. N. 2001. *The True African: Impulses for Self-affirmation*, Enugu Nigeria: Snaap Press.

Mcmurray, D. A. 2001. *In and Out of Morocco*, London: University of Minnesota Press.

Mgbeafulu, M. C. 2003. *Migration and the Economy*, New York: iUniverse Inc.

Moorehead, C. 2006. *Human Cargo*, London: Vintage Books.

Ndiokwere, N. I. 1998. *Search for Greener Pastures: Igbo and African Experience*, USA: Morris Publishing.

O'Brien, D. J., and Shannon, T.A., (eds.). 1992. *Catholic Social Thought: The Documentary Heitage*, New York: Orbis Books.

Orji, M. O. 1999. *The History and Culture of the Igbo People*, Nkpor Onitsha, Nigeria: Jet Publishers.

Parsons, S.F., (ed.). 2006. *Studies in Christian Ethics*, London: Sage Publications.

Schultheis, M. 1988. *Our Best Kept Secret; The Rich Heritage of Catholic Social Teaching*, England: CAFOD.

Udeafor, I. N. 1994. *Inculturation, Path to African Christianity*, Enugu Nigeria: Snaap Press.

Winder, R. 2005. *Bloody Foreigners*, Great Britain: Little, Brown.

Zolberg, A.R. et al. (eds.). 1989. *Escape from Violence: Conflict and the Refugee Crisis in the Developing World*, Oxford: Oxford University Press.

Encyclopaedia

Encyclopaedia Americana, International Edition, Canada: Grolier Limited, 1976.

Encyclopaedia Britannica, 15th Edition, USA: Encyclopaedia Britannica, Inc.,2002.

Encyclopaedia Britannica, 2005 Ultimate Reference Suite, in DVD.

New Catholic Encyclopaedia, 2nd edition, Vol. 13, Washington D.C.: Thomson Gale, 2003.

Internet Sources

http://www.unhchr.ch/html/menu6, 29.3.07.

http://www.religious.org/interdocs/docs/cairohislam1990.htm, 5.4.2007.

http://crawfurd.dk/africa/woed.htm, 5.4.2007.

http://www.jicef.or.jp/wahec/ful217.htm, 21.5.2007.

http://www.bridgewater.edu/~mtembo/africantraditionalfamily.htm, 21.5.2007.

http://family.jrank.org/pages/1613/South-Africa-Family-Life-in-BlackCommunities.htm, 21.5.2007.

http://www.ff.unily.si/oddleki/geo/publikacihe/dela/file/dela_21/033, 21.5.2007.

http://www.ngex.com/nigeria/places/states/enugu.htm, 22.9.2007.

http://www.cbc.ca/includes/printablestory.jsp, 3.10.2007.

http://edition.cnn.com/2005/WORLD/europe/11/10/france.riots/index.html, 3.10.2007.

http://www.unhr.org/cgibin/texis/vtx/protect/opendoc.pdf?tbi=PROTECTIONaid=3b66c2aalo, 28.06.2007.

http://www.ambafrance.org/news/statmnts/2006/euro_african_conference_Sarkozy, 610.2007.

http://news.yahoo.com/s/mcclatchy/20070905bcmoroccoimmigration_attn_national_f, 6.10.2007.

http://yaleglobal.yale.edu/display.article?id=7473, 3.10.2007.

http://www.miamiherald.comnewsworldv.prints/story/256345.html, 5.10.2007.

http://www.channel4.com/news/articles/general/water_cooler_moments/immigrants%,5.10.2007.

http://www.migrationinformation.org/Feature/display.cfm?id=483, 6.10.2007.

Newspapers, Articles and Magazines

'TIPPS', Austrian Newspaper.

Der Spiegel, Das Deutsche Nachrichten-Magazin, Nr.26/.26.6.06.

The New Partnership for Africa's Development, No.14, Justice and Peace Department of the South African Catholic Bishop's Conference, 2002.

Journal of Markets and Morality, No.1., Spring 2000.

People on the Move, XXXVIII, August, 2006.

Message of the Holy Father for the 87th World Day of Migration 2001.

Message of Benedict XVI, at the XVII plenary session of the PCPCM & I, 2006.

Interviews

Bakko, Nassara, 44 years old man from Nigeria. Living since 1992 in Linz, Upper Austria.

Njom, Tombia, a 56 years old man from Ghana. Living since 1990 in Linz, Upper Austria.

Church's Documents

Cathechism of the Catholic Church, Vaticana Libreria Editrice, 1992 (English Edition).

Flannery, A., Vatican II Council. The Conciliar and Post Conciliar Documents, Vol. 1, Vatican City: Dominican Publications, 1998.

Social Encyclicals

John XXIII, Mate et Magistra, 1961.

John XXIII, Pacem in Terris, 1963.

John Paul II, Laborem Exercens, 1981.

John Paul II, Sollicitudo Rei Socialis, 1987.

Leo XIII, Rerum Novarum, 1891.

Paul VI, Populorum Progressio, 1971.

Paul VI, Octogesima Adveniens, 1971.

Pius XII, Exsul Familia, 1952.

APPENDICES

Appendix 1: Summary of the Work in German

Einführung

Die Fähigkeit sich zu bewegen macht das Wesen lebender Organismen aus. Ein(Aus)wanderung wird durch viele Faktoren verursacht, angefangen von den bewundernswertesten bis zu den unklarsten (unverständlichsten). Die Menschen haben sich diese Fähigkeit mehr als irgendein anderes Lebewesen auf der Erde zunutze gemacht, um sich einerseits den sich ständig verändernden Situationen anzupassen, oder auch, um gegen die Bedrohungen ihrer Existenz anzukämpfen. Solche Bedrohungen sind für gewöhnlich entweder direkt oder indirekt mit ihrem Leben verbunden. Das ist das, was man in der Fachsprache als Migration bezeichnet. Im Verlauf der Migration machen Menschen Gebrauch von verschiedensten Beförderungsmitteln. Die Straßen sind blockiert von einer Menge von Fahrzeugen, die Eisenbahnen und Flughäfen sind überfüllt mit Menschen, die von einem Ort zum anderen gebracht werden. Sogar in den Wüsten findet man Spuren derer, die hier einen Weg der Migration suchen.

Es ist eine bekannte Tatsache, dass Menschen immer in Bewegung sind. Sie bewegen sich nicht nur hin und her, oder von Ort zu Ort, sie sind auch mit ihrem Gepäck in Bewegung. Eigentlich kann man nicht zu einer Reise aufbrechen ohne die geringste Erwartung zu haben, unterwegs andere zu treffen, und zahllose Menschen versuchen irgendwohin zu kommen.

Die Völkerwanderung kann wie folgt in zwei Kategorien eingeteilt werden: freiwillige und erzwungene. Die Fortbewegungsmethode des Einzelnen definiert manchmal die Kategorie solch einer Auswanderung. Diejenigen, die gezwungen werden auszuwandern, verdienen große Aufmerksamkeit. Das sind die Menschen, die ihre Heimat verlassen oder aus ihrer Heimat vertrieben werden, und die aufgrund dessen möglicherweise vielleicht verschleppt werden. Oft bleibt ihr Weggehen unbeachtet , da sich viele an die Unterseite von fahrenden Zügen klammern, oder erfroren gefunden werden in den Rädern von Flugzeugen, oder sie kriechen in der Dunkelheit durch Tunnels oder werden wie Sardinen in Schiffe geschlichtet. Viele dieser Zwangsmigranten fallen aufgrund ihres mangelnden Wissens/ihrer mangelnden Erfahrung in die Hände von Betrügern/Schleppern und riskieren somit ihr schon bedrohtes Leben. Viele enden auf diese Art im Elend, während andere es zu etwas bringen/schaffen.

Aber wenn Menschen weggehen von einem Ort, treffen sie auf diesem Weg andere, die ankommen.

Das Paradox der Migration wirft die Frage nach der Nationalität auf, wenn die Grenzen eines bestimmten Landes überschritten werden. Politische Immigrationsmaßnahmen sind gefordert. Wenn eine internationale Bewegung legal ist, dann sollte ein gültiges vorgeschriebenes Visum vorgelegt werden, ansonsten werden Migranten als illegal bezeichnet. Das ist gut und notwendig, aber wir dürfen nicht vergessen, dass es Menschen gibt, die auf Grund von Katastrophen und verschiedenster Bedrohungen gezwungen sind ihre Heimat zu verlassen auch ohne ein Visum zu besitzen.

Ziel dieser Arbeit ist es, Korrekturen und Verbesserungsvorschläge zu machen, die diese Kurzsichtigkeit betreffen. Weiters geht es auch um die Aufklärung und Schaffung eines Leidensbewusstseins dieser so genannten illegalen Migranten und der Migranten im Allgemeinen.

Ohne Vorurteil gegenüber den Migranten mit gültigen Visas- alle, die in ein anderes Land, das nicht ihr Heimatland ist, einwandern, werden als Fremde eingestuft (kategorisiert). Für diejenigen, die kein gültiges Visum besitzen, ist die Deportation die nächste Alternative der Regierung/Behörde, ausgenommen wenn sie den Status eines Asylanten oder Flüchtlings haben oder sich in einem laufenden Verfahren befinden. Auf jeden Fall existiert eine zunehmende Spannung zwischen den Migranten, die sich legal oder illegal in einem Land befinden und jenen, die Staatsbürger dieses Landes sind.

Das Hauptinteresse dieser Arbeit gilt den afrikanischen Migranten, die nach Europa kommen. Viele von ihnen sind gesetzlich anerkannt, noch weit mehr sind die, die es nicht sind.

In dieser Arbeit werden wir versuchen einen Überblick über die Situation zu geben und eine Bewertung/ein Urteil abzugeben.

Migration und die Suche nach Anerkennung als Asylant oder Flüchtling sind zu einem beständigen Problem in den letzten Jahrzehnten geworden.

Man ist diesen Menschen immer mit Unverständnis/Unsicherheit begegnet, manchmal ist dies jedoch von ihnen selbst verursacht durch ihr Verhalten. Für beide gilt, dass die Art ihres Verhaltens anderen gegenüber eine Hauptsorge ist.

Ungeachtet dessen, sind wir aufgerufen, als Geschöpfe Gottes miteinander respektvoll und achtsam umzugehen und die Wurzeln der Freundschaft zu finden, die Angst und Ablehnung besiegen, die immer wieder das ruhige, angenehme Leben stören.

Es soll angemerkt werden, dass diese Einwanderer Menschen sind. Unser Verhalten in der zwischenmenschlichen Beziehung mit ihnen soll beruhen auf Liebe, Toleranz, Verständnis und Achtsamkeit. Menschen sollten als Menschen gesehen, betrachtet und als Menschen behandelt werden und nicht als „Dinge“, die als Nebenprodukte einer äußerst schlimmen Bewegung in der Welt, Migration genannt, weggeworfen werden.

Aufbau der Arbeit

Diese Arbeit ist in fünf Kapiteln unterteilt.

Im ersten Kapitel versuchten wir eine praktische Definition und eine Erklärung/Erläuterung der wichtigsten Schlüsselbegriffe zu geben wie: Migration, Asylanten und Flüchtlinge. Die versuchten Definitionen in diesem Kapitel stellen nur eine Annäherung an die Themen dar, die auf dem begrenzten Gebiet unserer Arbeit basieren. Sie sind klar begrenzt und definiert im Hinblick auf die Art ihrer unterschiedlichen Ansprüche. Das Ergebnis ist, dass diese Forderungen in großem Maß helfen, die politischen Themen, die das Thema Migration, Asylanten und Flüchtlinge betreffen einer ethischen Prüfung zu unterziehen. In diesem Kapitel definierten wir den Asylwerber als jemanden der aufgrund von Verfolgung und Anschläge auf sein Leben gezwungen war die Heimat zu verlasse. Als Flüchtlinge werden jene Personen angesehen die aufgrund einer momentanen Gefahr ihre Heimat verlassen.

Es gibt Ähnlichkeiten aber der gravierende Unterschied zwischen den beiden ist, dass der Asylwerber vor Verfolgung flieht. In diesem Kapitel zitierten wir die Definition zum Thema Migranten unter Berücksichtigung der Menschenrechtserklärung und ihre Anwendung als Paradigma.

Der Flüchtling entflieht nicht unbedingt der Verfolgung sondern kann in seiner Heimat zurückkehren sobald die Bedrohung bzw. Katastrophe vorüber ist. Beide jedoch, Asylwerber wie auch Flüchtlinge, suchen Schutz weil ihr Leben bedroht wird.

Wir setzten fort im 2. Kapitel mit der Untersuchung der Situation in Afrika. Das soll uns ein klares und allgemeines Bild dieses Kontinents vermitteln von dem die euro-afrikanischen Migranten stammen. Es ist sachdienlich anzumerken, dass das Bild der afrikanischen Gesellschaft hier nicht im Detail beschrieben wird. Nur diese Aspekte, die für uns zweckdienlich sind, wurden untersucht mit dem Ziel, diese Aspekte später hervorzuheben als einen Teil der Gründe, warum Migranten von ihrer Heimat weggehen. Außerdem haben wir uns in unserer Arbeit auf die gesellschaftliche Situation in Nigeria konzentriert, das die bevölkerungsreichste multi-ethische Nation Afrikas ist.

Im dritten Kapitel kamen wir zu den konkreten Gründen, die die Aus/Ein wanderung von Menschen als Flüchtlinge oder Asylanten nach

Europa notwendig machen. Wenn man dem Diktat/Aussagen der Menschenrechte und dem natürlichen Instinkt des Menschen folgt, gibt es eine Rechtfertigung für die Migration der Menschen. Eine Rechtfertigung, die verstärkt wird durch die Tatsache, dass das Recht auf Leben unveräußerlich ist und es zum Menschen als Mensch gehört. Wir versuchten auch die verschiedenen Probleme denen afrikanische Immigranten in den jeweiligen europäischen Ländern ausgesetzt sind, näher zu beleuchten.

Diese Probleme treten hauptsächlich in den Bereichen Kultur, Mentalität, Sprache, Rassismus, Ausgrenzung und Anfeindung auf. Es sind offensichtliche Faktoren die es schon immer gab und die große Schwierigkeiten für Afrikaner in Europa darstellen. In diesem Kapitel drei schauten wir uns die verschiedenen Probleme von Migranten an, und wir versuchten die Situation in Frankreich und Spanien genauer zu betrachten. Wir vertieften uns in dieses Thema, weil es um die Erhaltung von Leben geht, und wenn es gefährdet ist, gibt es das Recht, es zu schützen. Hunger und Verfolgung können das Leben bedrohen und wenn diese unmittelbar bevorstehen, dann ist das Beste, was man tun kann, wegzugehen. Das ist die Situation in den meisten afrikanischen Ländern.

In Kapitel 4 dieser Arbeit befassten wir uns mit den Stellungnahmen der Kirche und einiger Sozialenzykliken, die dieses Thema behandeln. Wir versuchen die Prinzipien der „Catholic Social Teaching“ zu analysieren. In diesem Kapitel wurde die Entwicklung des sozialen Unterrichts und ihre Ausmaße nachverfolgt. Solidarität, die als zentrales Thema der Enzyklika „Sollicitudo Rei Socialis“ zutage tritt, fungiert als relevante Grundlage in dieser Enzyklika für Probleme der Immigranten, Asylwerber und Flüchtlinge.

Kapitel 5 beendet die Arbeit mit einer kritischen Evaluation und einer allgemeinen Bewertung/Beurteilung der Lage/Situation. In diesem letzten Abschnitt der Arbeit versuchten wir die ethischen, praktischen und sozialen Erfahrungen der vorhergehenden Kapitel zusammenzubringen, um zu einer kritischen Bewertung dieser Arbeit zu kommen. Schließlich ist es wichtig anzumerken, dass das Thema dieser Arbeit ein beständiges/aktuelles Problem in der Welt der Politik und der wirtschaftlich-sozialen Ordnung ist. Was Moral betrifft, muss die Kirche in dieser Richtung die Rolle eines „wachsamen Hundes" spielen.

Da es ein riesiges Gebiet und ein aktuelles Thema des 21. Jahrhunderts ist, können wir nicht behaupten, den ganzen Bereich in Kurzfassung abgedeckt zu haben. Aber das Ziel der ganzen Arbeit ist, die ungerechtfertigte Art jedes Versuchs aufzuzeigen, der auf Verunmöglichung von Migration abzielt in der Weise, dass er nicht basiert auf dem Beweggrund des Allgemeinwohles und weiters die unmenschliche Behandlung jener Migranten anzuprangern, die wegen der Situation in ihren Heimatländern zu Bürgern keines Landes gemacht werden.

Was wir in dieser Arbeit versucht haben zu tun, ist, die Herausforderungen zu analysieren, denen sich die ganze Welt stellen muss in Bezug auf die ethisch vorbildliche Antwort gegenüber Flüchtlingen und Asylwerbern auf der ganzen Welt. In diesem Kapitel beschreiben wir die rechtliche Grundlage. Bei dem Versuch diese Arbeit zu bewerten stellten wir fest dass ein Land nicht die Möglichkeiten besitzt sämtlichen sich bewerbenden Immigranten aufzunehmen. Dies stellt natürlich ein rechtliches Problem dar. Zu dem kommt noch hinzu dass, falls zu viele Immigranten in einem Land aufgenommen werden, das soziale und kulturelle Leben der Einwohner in der Folge darunter zu leiden hätte.

Aus den praktischen Erfahrungen verschiedener Nationen und der Relevanz der Lehre der Kirche auf diesem Gebiet folgernd, versuchten wir in einer gemäßigten Weise auf dieses Phänomen eine Antwort zu geben.

Epilog

Die Prinzipien echten Humanismus können sogar angesichts echt empfundener Solidarität missverstanden und falsch angewendet werden. Das ist die Situation mit dem Problem/Ergebnis eines offensichtlichen Bemühens, das aufzeigen soll, dass es nicht notwendig ist für Afrikaner auszuwandern.

Migration ist ein Problem des 21. Jahrhunderts. Es ist schon immer ein Problem gewesen, aber nicht in diesem Ausmaß wie es im 21.Jahrhundert, der Fall ist. Das Thema/Problem der Asylwerber, Flüchtlinge und Migranten ist ein ernstzunehmendes Thema in letzter Zeit.

Wie wir schon erwähnt haben, hat es immer Menschen gegeben, die unterwegs waren, sich aus verschiedenen Gründen in ihrem Land hin und her bewegten, was man zusammenfassend als ‚Suche nach Leben' bezeichnen kann. Schon seit dem 16.Jahrhundert waren Menschen unterwegs zur Arbeit, zu erforschen, zu reisen, besseres Leben zu finden. Was niemand so ganz vorhersah, war die Entstehung neuer multikultureller Gesellschaften und auch nicht die neuen Strukturen, die Migration angenommen hat.

In dieser Arbeit haben wir versucht für einen Standpunkt/eine Haltung einzutreten, der/die zweierlei erreichen sollte: Vermeidung einer selbstsüchtigen Spezifizierung und eines unterdrückenden Liberalismus; und die Erkenntnis des Einsseins, was Menschlichkeit anbelangt, und Solidarität in der Entwicklung.

Dass es immer noch Menschen in der Welt gibt, die trotz der Schwierigkeiten, die illegale Migration nach sich zieht, die Grenze in ein anderes Land überschreiten möchten, sogar unter Einsatz ihres Lebens, ist ein Zeichen, dass etwas falsch läuft in der Welt.

Der Mangel an Solidarität, wie sie Papst Johannes Paul II in der Enzyklika Sollicitudo Rei Socialis angedeutet hat, ist ein Faktor, mit dem man rechnen muss in dieser Richtung.

Die Länder der entwickelten Welt werden schuldig wegen ihrer egoistischen Sonderbestrebungen, wenn sie nur das eigene Wohl im Auge haben indem sie den anderen die Tür verschließen.

Das Allgemeinwohl, dem jedes Gesetz dienen sollte, weitet sich aus bis zu einem gewissen Grad auf die anderen Mitglieder der Menschheitsfamilie.

Wenn man weiß, dass diese Migranten entweder einer meist durch die Regierung verursachten Verfolgung entkommen oder aus lebensbedrohlichen Situationen flüchten, dann wird es eine Handlung gegen Moral und Heiligkeit des Lebens sie in dieses System zurückzuschicken, das sie eigentlich umbringen will.

Manchmal gibt es Situationen, in denen Migranten eine Menge Lügen erzählen und Fälle von Verfolgung und Bedrohung ihres Lebens erfinden.

Wie Moorehead es sagt: „Ich begann mit keiner vorgefassten Meinung, außer einer Bestätigung, dass es unter den Asylwerbern sicherlich Leute gibt, die keine Verfolgungsgeschichte haben und dass nicht alles, was sie mir sagten, wahr sein würde."

Darum sollte es genaue Vorgangsweisen im Umgang mit den Themen, die Migranten betreffen, geben, indem man bedenkt, dass Missbrauch nicht die weitere Anwendung verhindert.

In diesem Zusammenhang sollte die Arbeit von dem, der das Interview leitet um zu bestimmen, wer den Status eines Asylwerbers bekommt und wer nicht, nicht nur darin bestehen, nach Lügen und Widersprüchlichkeiten in den Aussagen der Asylanten zu suchen.

Einige Länder lassen Migranten zu wegen der billigen Arbeitskraft. Verzweifelte und Verwundbare sind bereit, jeden Job für jeden Preis zu machen und manchmal auch nur für Essen.

Es wird ein unterdrückender Liberalismus, wenn diese Migranten willkommen geheißen werden mit der Absicht sie auszubeuten. Die meisten arbeiten und leben unter äußerst erniedrigenden Umständen in überfüllten Häusern oder manchmal in improvisierten Lagern. Ihnen wird im Allgemeinen der Zugang zu legaler Hilfe und Ausbildung verwehrt. Diejenigen, die illegal in der Wirtschaft arbeiten wie in Spanien und Italien, sind genau so Gegenstand schlimmer Ausbeutung und eines Missbrauchs durch ihre Arbeitgeber. Es ist auch möglich, dass die Regierung unter Druck kommt durch die Forderung der Unternehmer nach Hilfsarbeitern, was darauf schließen lässt, dass man mehr legalen Einwanderern erlaubt zu kommen , oder dass die legalisiert werden, die bereits drinnen sind.

Die Kirche versucht, die Menschen zur einen vollen Verwirklichung ihrer Rolle als Baumeister der menschlichen Gesellschaft zu führen, Vertreter von Entwicklung und Verfechter von Solidarität untereinander zu sein.

Dass auf dem Recht auf wirtschaftliche Initiative ständig herumgetrampelt wird, ist eine bekannte Tatsache, und das ist eines der Rechte, das allen nutzen würde, wenn es richtig gehandhabt würde.

In einem unbewussten Befolgen der Anweisungen der Enzyklika Sollicitudo Rei Socialis handeln die meisten Länder der Welt in einer positiven Weise, um das Leiden dieser illegalen Einwanderer zu lindern. Manchmal begegnet man dem Missmut anderer Länder.

In Afrika wird Algerien öffentlich von Marokko beschuldigt, dass es den 'sub-Saharans' stillschweigend erlaubt über ihr Territorium auszuwandern.

In Europa wird Spanien beschuldigt, im Jahr 2005 über 600.000 Migranten gesetzlich anerkannt zu haben, was möglicherweise mehr Illegale anzieht. Spanien hat diese Reaktion ‚demagogisch' genannt und hat aufgezeigt, dass in der Vergangenheit die meisten EU Mitgliedsstaaten sich gezwungen sahen, auf ähnliche Einbindungen/ Anerkennungen ihrer de facto fixen/festgelegten, nicht dokumentierten Arbeitskräfte zurückzugreifen.

Wenn man der Komplexität dieser Problematik folgt, wird ein hartes Vorgehen, das darauf abzielt, den Menschenhandel zu verhindern immer auf irgendwelche Hindernisse stoßen.

Die Lösung wird eher eine stillschweigende Maßnahme sein, die eher eine Kontrolle braucht als eine Aufhebung. Es muss basieren auf einer gemeinsamen Zusammenarbeit aller Nationen in der Entwicklung der Welt.

In dem Wissen und in dem Spüren, dass die Welt miteinander verbunden ist in einem gemeinsamen Schicksal, sollten die Nationen auch zusammenarbeiten.

Die Souveränität eines Landes sollte von allen anerkannt werden. Und die illegalen Einwanderer müssen ihren Teil dazu beitragen in dieser Forderung nach Respekt als sie natürlich reagieren auf den menschlichen Instinkt Leben zu bewahren.

Wenn die Nationen und die Menschen der Welt es nicht schaffen im Geist/Sinn der Solidarität zusammenzuarbeiten, kann nichts von dem, was in dieser Arbeit angeregt/vorgeschlagen oder untersucht wurde, erreicht werden.

Mit dem Verstehen des Terminus „Solidarität" wie es in Sollicitudo Rei Socialis verwendet und empfohlen wird in Bezug auf die Entwicklung der Welt, kann die Autonomie des Menschen in einem gewissen Ausmaß erreicht werden, weil Solidarität die Bereitschaft fordert, auch Opfer anzunehmen, die notwendig sind für das Wohl der ganzen Welt-Gemeinschaft.

Alle Menschen sehnen sich nach einem besseren Leben, daran sollten die Nationen denken.

Es kann nicht geleugnet werden, dass es gut wäre, wenn Situationen, die Migration nötig machen, gar nicht erst auftauchen würden. Wenn das passiert, werden die Menschen aufhören auszuwandern. Und jene, die schon ausgewandert sind, werden heimkommen. Aber bis der mögliche Tag kommt, wenn sie heimkehren können, werden Flüchtlinge weiterhin wegziehen und Regierungen haben keine Alternative, außer politische Maßnahmen zu finden, die ihre Grenzen schützen, aber die auch menschlich sind und die Rechte derer schützen, die Asyl suchen.

Menschen zu schützen, die vor Verfolgung fliehen, ist eine Verantwortung, die alle Staaten teilen müssen, wenn kollektive Souveränität moralischen Wert haben soll. Die Kirche macht vieles in dieser Richtung.

Einen Migranten nicht zu akzeptieren, trägt dazu bei, dass sich seine Situation verschlechtert, besonders wenn er vor Verfolgung und Lebensbedrohung flieht.

Appendix 2: Figures

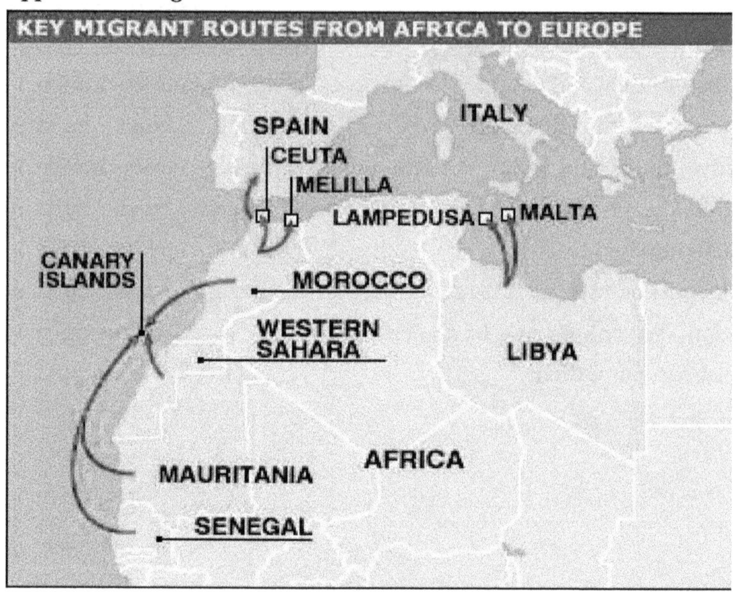

http://news.bbc.co.uk/2/hi/africa/6172184.stm

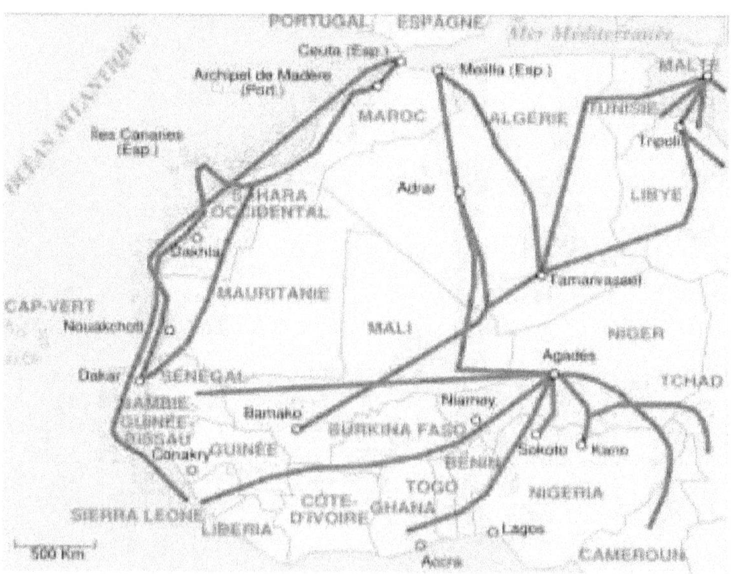

http://en.wikipedia.org/wiki/Migrants'_african_routes

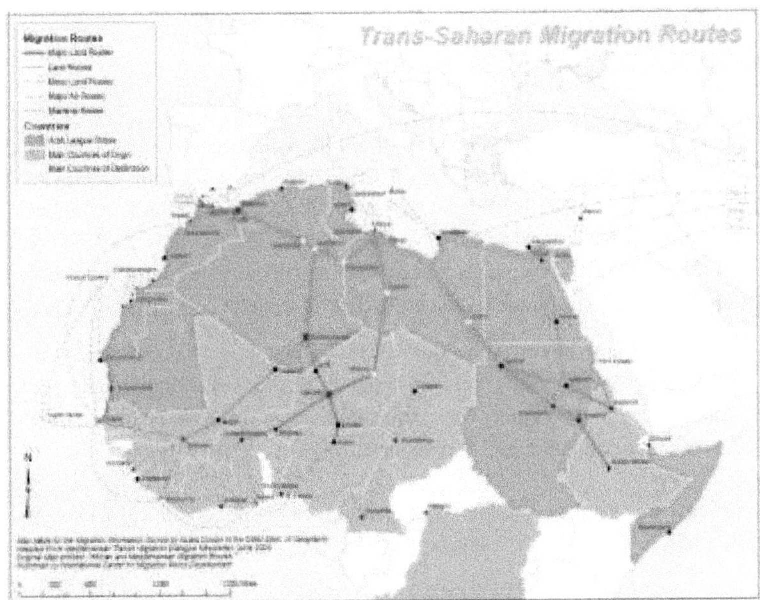

http://www.migrationinformation.org/Feature/display.cfm?ID=578

IMMIGRANTS IN EUROPE BY REGION OF ORIGIN 2005

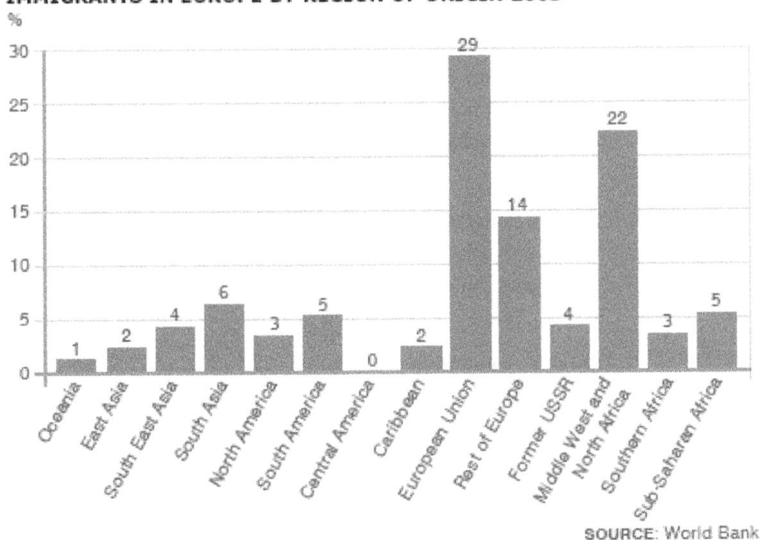

http://news.bbc.co.uk/2/hi/europe/6228236.

Globethics.net

Globethics.net is an ethics network of teachers and institutions based in Geneva, with an international Board of Foundation and with ECOSOC status with the United Nations. Our vision is to embed ethics in higher education. We strive for a world in which people, and especially leaders, are educated in, informed by and act according to ethical values and thus contribute to building sustainable, just and peaceful societies.

The founding conviction of Globethics.net is that having equal access to knowledge resources in the field of applied ethics enables individuals and institutions from developing and transition economies to become more visible and audible in the global discourse.

In order to ensure access to knowledge resources in applied ethics, Globethics.net has developed four resources:

Globethics.net Library
The leading global digital library on ethics with over 8 million documents and specially curated content

Globethics.net Publications
A publishing house open to all the authors interested in applied ethics and with over 190 publications in 15 series

Globethics.net Academy
Online and offline courses and training for all on ethics both as a subject and within specific sectors

Globethics.net Network
A global network of experts and institutions including a Pool of experts and a Consortium

Globethics.net provides an electronic platform for dialogue, reflection and action. Its central instrument is the website:

www.globethics.net ▪

Globethics.net Publications

The list below is only a selection of our publications. To view the full collection, please visit our website.

All products are provided free of charge and can be downloaded in PDF form from the Globethics.net library and at www.globethics.net/publications. Bulk print copies can be ordered from *publictions@globethics.net* at special rates for those from the Global South.
Paid products not provided free of charge are indicated*.
The Editor of the different Series of Globethics.net Publications is Prof. Dr Obiora Ike, Executive Director of Globethics.net in Geneva and Professor of Ethics at the Godfrey Okoye University Enugu/Nigeria.

Contact for manuscripts and suggestions: *publications@globethics.net*

Global Series

Christoph Stückelberger / Jesse N.K. Mugambi (eds.), *Responsible Leadership. Global and Contextual Perspectives*, 2007, 376pp. ISBN: 978–2–8254–1516–0

Heidi Hadsell / Christoph Stückelberger (eds.), *Overcoming Fundamentalism. Ethical Responses from Five Continents*, 2009, 212pp. ISBN: 978–2–940428–00–7

Christoph Stückelberger / Reinhold Bernhardt (eds.): *Calvin Global. How Faith Influences Societies*, 2009, 258pp. ISBN: 978–2–940428–05–2.

Ariane Hentsch Cisneros / Shanta Premawardhana (eds.), *Sharing Values. A Hermeneutics for Global Ethics*, 2010, 418pp. ISBN: 978–2–940428–25–0.

Deon Rossouw / Christoph Stückelberger (eds.), *Global Survey of Business Ethics in Training, Teaching and Research*, 2012, 404pp. ISBN: 978–2–940428–39–7

Carol Cosgrove Sacks/ Paul H. Dembinski (eds.), *Trust and Ethics in Finance. Innovative Ideas from the Robin Cosgrove Prize*, 2012, 380pp. ISBN: 978–2–940428–41–0

Jean-Claude Bastos de Morais / Christoph Stückelberger (eds.), *Innovation Ethics. African and Global Perspectives*, 2014, 233pp. ISBN: 978–2–88931–003–6

Nicolae Irina / Christoph Stückelberger (eds.), *Mining, Ethics and Sustainability*, 2014, 198pp. ISBN: 978–2–88931–020–3

Philip Lee and Dafne Sabanes Plou (eds), *More or Less Equal: How Digital Platforms Can Help Advance Communication Rights*, 2014, 158pp. ISBN 978–2–88931–009–8

Sanjoy Mukherjee and Christoph Stückelberger (eds.) *Sustainability Ethics. Ecology, Economy, Ethics. International Conference SusCon III, Shillong/India*, 2015, 353pp. ISBN: 978–2–88931–068–5

Amélie Vallotton Preisig / Hermann Rösch / Christoph Stückelberger (eds.) *Ethical Dilemmas in the Information Society. Codes of Ethics for Librarians and Archivists*, 2014, 224pp. ISBN: 978–288931–024–1.

Prospects and Challenges for the Ecumenical Movement in the 21st Century. Insights from the Global Ecumenical Theological Institute, David Field / Jutta Koslowski, 256pp. 2016, ISBN: 978–2–88931–097–5

Christoph Stückelberger, Walter Fust, Obiora Ike (eds.), *Global Ethics for Leadership. Values and Virtues for Life,* 2016, 444pp. ISBN: 978–2–88931–123–1

Dietrich Werner / Elisabeth Jeglitzka (eds.), *Eco-Theology, Climate Justice and Food Security: Theological Education and Christian Leadership Development*, 316pp. 2016, ISBN 978–2–88931–145–3

Obiora Ike, Andrea Grieder and Ignace Haaz (Eds.), *Poetry and Ethics: Inventing Possibilities in Which We Are Moved to Action and How We Live Together*, 271pp. 2018, ISBN 978–2–88931–242–9

Christoph Stückelberger / Pavan Duggal (Eds.), *Cyber Ethics 4.0: Serving Humanity with Values*, 503pp. 2018, ISBN 978–2–88931–264-1

Texts Series

Principles on Sharing Values across Cultures and Religions, 2012, 20pp. Available in English, French, Spanish, German and Chinese. Other languages in preparation. ISBN: 978–2–940428–09–0

Ethics in Politics. Why it Matters More than Ever and How it Can Make a Difference. A Declaration, 8pp, 2012. Available in English and French. ISBN: 978–2–940428–35–9

Religions for Climate Justice: International Interfaith Statements 2008–2014, 2014, 45pp. Available in English. ISBN 978–2–88931–006–7

Ethics in the Information Society: The Nine 'P's. A Discussion Paper for the WSIS+10 Process 2013–2015, 2013, 32pp. ISBN: 978–2–940428–063–2

Principles on Equality and Inequality for a Sustainable Economy. Endorsed by the Global Ethics Forum 2014 with Results from Ben Africa Conference 2014, 2015, 41pp. ISBN: 978–2–88931–025–8

Water Ethics: Principles and Guidelines, 2019, 41pp. ISBN 978–2–88931-313-6, available in three languages.

Praxis Series

Christoph Stückelberger, *Responsible Leadership Handbook : For Staff and Boards*, 2014, 116pp. ISBN :978-2-88931-019-7 (Available in Russian)

Angèle Kolouchè Biao, Aurélien Atidegla (éds.,) *Proverbes du Bénin. Sagesse éthique appliquée de proverbes africains*, 2015, 132pp. ISBN 978-2-88931-068-5

Elly K. Kansiime, *In the Shadows of Truth: The Polarized Family*, 2017, 172pp. ISBN 978-2-88931-203-0

Christopher Byaruhanga, *Essential Approaches to Christian Religious Education: Learning and Teaching in Uganda*, 2018, 286pp. ISBN: 978-2-88931-235-1

Christoph Stückelberger / William Otiende Ogara / Bright Mawudor, *African Church Assets Handbook*, 2018, 291pp. ISBN: 978-2-88931-252-8

Oscar Brenifier, *Day After Day 365 Aphorisms*, 2019, 395pp. ISBN 978-2-88931-272-6

Christoph Stückelberger, *365 Way-Markers*, 2019, 416pp. ISBN: 978-2-88931-282-5 (available in English and German).

Benoît Girardin / Evelyne Fiechter-Widemann (Eds.), *Blue Ethics: Ethical Perspectives on Sustainable, Fair Water Resources Use and Management*, forthcoming 2019, 265pp. ISBN 978-2-88931-308-2

Elly Kansiime, *Theology of Work and Development*, 158pp. 2020, ISBN 978-2-88931-373-0

Theses Series

Kitoka Moke Mutondo, *Église, protection des droits de l'homme et refondation de l'État en République Démocratique du Congo*, 2012, 412pp. ISBN: 978–2–940428–31–1

Ange Sankieme Lusanga, *Éthique de la migration. La valeur de la justice comme base pour une migration dans l'Union Européenne et la Suisse*, 2012, 358pp. ISBN: 978–2–940428–49–6

Kahwa Njojo, *Éthique de la non-violence*, 2013, 596pp.
ISBN: 978–2–940428–61–8

Carlos Alberto Sintado, *Social Ecology, Ecojustice and the New Testament: Liberating Readings,* 2015, 379pp. ISBN: 978-2–940428–99–1

Symphorien Ntibagirirwa, *Philosophical Premises for African Economic Development: Sen's Capability Approach*, 2014, 384pp.
ISBN: 978–2–88931–001–2

Jude Likori Omukaga, *Right to Food Ethics: Theological Approaches of Asbjørn Eide,* 2015, 609pp. ISBN: 978–2–88931–047–0

Jörg F. W. Bürgi, *Improving Sustainable Performance of SME's, The Dynamic Interplay of Morality and Management Systems*, 2014, 528pp.
ISBN: 978–2–88931–015–9

Jun Yan, *Local Culture and Early Parenting in China: A Case Study on Chinese Christian Mothers' Childrearing Experiences,* 2015, 190pp.
ISBN 978–2–88931–065–4

Frédéric-Paul Piguet, *Justice climatique et interdiction de nuire*, 2014, 559 pp.
ISBN 978–2–88931–005–0

Mulolwa Kashindi, *Appellations johanniques de Jésus dans l'Apocalypse: une lecture Bafuliiru des titres christologiques*, 2015, 577pp. ISBN 978–2–88931–040–1

Naupess K. Kibiswa, *Ethnonationalism and Conflict Resolution: The Armed Group Bany2 in DR Congo.* 2015, 528pp. ISBN: 978–2–88931–032–6

Kilongo Fatuma Ngongo, *Les héroïnes sans couronne. Leadership des femmes dans les Églises de Pentecôte en Afrique Centrale,* 2015, 489pp. ISBN 978–2–88931–038–8

Bosela E. Eale, *Justice and Poverty as Challenges for Churches: with a Case Study of the Democratic Republic of Congo*, 2015, 335pp,
ISBN: 978–2–88931–078–4

Andrea Grieder, *Collines des mille souvenirs. Vivre* après *et* avec *le génocide perpétré contre les Tutsi du Rwanda,* 2016, 403pp. ISBN 978–2–88931–101–9

Monica Emmanuel, *Federalism in Nigeria: Between Divisions in Conflict and Stability in Diversity*, 2016, 522pp. ISBN: 978–2–88931–106–4

John Kasuku, *Intelligence Reform in the Post-Dictatorial Democratic Republic of Congo*, 2016, 355pp. ISBN 978–2–88931–121–7

Fifamè Fidèle Houssou Gandonour, *Les fondements éthiques du féminisme. Réflexions à partir du contexte africain*, 2016, 430pp. ISBN 978–2–88931–138–5

Nicoleta Acatrinei, *Work Motivation and Pro-Social Behaviour in the Delivery of Public Services Theoretical and Empirical Insights*, 2016, 387pp. ISBN 978–2–88931–150–7

Timothee B. Mushagalusa, *John of Damascus and Heresy. A Basis for Understanding Modern Heresy*, 2017, 556pp. ISBN: 978-2-88931-205-4

Nina, Mariani Noor, *Ahmadi Women Resisting Fundamentalist Persecution. A Case Study on Active Group Resistance in Indonesia*, 2018, 221pp. ISBN: 978-2-88931-222-1

Ernest Obodo, Christian *Education in Nigeria and Ethical Challenges. Context of Enugu Diocese*, 2018, 612pp. ISBN: 978-2-88931-256-6

Fransiska Widyawati, *Catholics in Manggarai, Flores, Eastern Indonesia,* 2018, 284pp. ISBN: 978-2-88931-268-9

A. Halil Thahir, *Ijtihād Maqāṣidi: The Interconnected Maṣlaḥah-Based Reconstruction of Islamic Laws,* 2019, 200pp. ISBN 978-2-88931-220-7*10*

Tibor Héjj, *Human Dignity in Managing Employees. A performative approach, based on the Catholic Social Teaching (CST),* 2019, 320pp. ISBN: 978-2-88931-280-1

Sabina Kavutha Mutisya, *The Experience of Being a Divorced or Separated Single Mother: A Phenomenological Study,* 2019, 168pp. ISBN: 978-2-88931-274-0

Florence Muia, *Sustainable Peacebuilding Strategies. Sustainable Peacebuilding Operations in Nakuru County, Kenya: Contribution to the Catholic Justice and Peace Commission (CJPC),* 2020, 195pp. ISBN: 978-2-88931-331-0

Mary Rose-Claret Ogbuehi, *The Struggle for Women Empowerment Through Education,* 2020, 410pp. ISBN: 978-2-88931-363-1

Nestor Engone Elloué, *La justice climatique restaurative: Réparer les inégalités Nord/Sud*, 2020, 198pp. ISBN 978-2-88931-379-2

Hilary C. Ike, *Organizational Improvement of Nigerian Catholic Chaplaincy in Central Ohio: Towards Effective Collaboration for Rural and Community Development in Nigeria – Ethical Considerations*, 154pp. 2021, ISBN 978-2-88931-385-3

Education Ethics Series

Divya Singh / Christoph Stückelberger (Eds.), *Ethics in Higher Education Values-driven Leaders for the Future,* 2017, 367pp. ISBN: 978–2–88931–165–1

Obiora Ike / Chidiebere Onyia (Eds.) *Ethics in Higher Education, Foundation for Sustainable Development*, 2018, 645pp. IBSN: 978-2-88931-217-7

Obiora Ike / Chidiebere Onyia (Eds.) *Ethics in Higher Education, Religions and Traditions in Nigeria* 2018, 198pp. IBSN: 978-2-88931-219-1

Obiora F. Ike, Justus Mbae, Chidiebere Onyia (Eds.), *Mainstreaming Ethics in Higher Education: Research Ethics in Administration, Finance, Education, Environment and Law Vol. 1*, 2019, 779pp. ISBN 978-2-88931-300-6

Ikechukwu J. Ani/Obiora F. Ike (Eds.), *Higher Education in Crisis Sustaining Quality Assurance and Innovation in Research through Applied Ethics*, 2019, 214pp. ISBN 978-2-88931-323-5

Obiora Ike, Justus Mbae, Chidiebere Onyia, Herbert Makinda (Eds.), *Mainstreaming Ethics in Higher Education Vol. 2*, 2021, 420pp. ISBN: 978-2-88931-383-9

Ethical Sieve Series

Paul Dembinski, Josina Kamerling and Virgile Perret (Eds.), *Changing Frontiers of Ethics in Finance*, 2019, 511pp. ISBN 978-2-88931-317-4

Co-publications & Other

Kenneth R. Ross, *Mission Rediscovered: Transforming Disciples*, 2020, 138pp. ISBN 978-2-88931-369-3

Obiora Ike, Amélé Adamavi-Aho Ekué, Anja Andriamay, Lucy Howe López (Eds.), *Who Cares About Ethics? 2020*, 352pp. ISBN 978-2-88931-381-5

This is only selection of our latest publications, to view our full collection please visit:

www.globethics.net/publications

www.ingramcontent.com/pod-product-compliance
Ingram Content Group UK Ltd.
Pitfield, Milton Keynes, MK11 3LW, UK
UKHW021127260726
13994UKWH00001B/21

9 782889 313884